H
I Could Use a Little Help Here!

My Story of
Healthcare Workplace Violence

June Zanes Garen, RN

BURLINGTON,
VERMONT

Onion River Press
191 Bank Street
Burlington, VT 05401

Publisher's Cataloging-in-Publication data

Names: Garen, June Zanes, author.
Title: Hey! I could use a little help here ! My story of healthcare workplace violence / June Zanes Garen, RN.
Description: Burlington, VT: Onion River Press, 2021.
Identifiers: LCCN: 2021904289 | ISBN: 978-1-949066-72-2
Subjects: LCSH Garen, June Zanes. | Medical personnel--Violence against. | Violence in the workplace. | Post-traumatic stress disorder. | BISAC BIOGRAPHY & AUTOBIOGRAPHY / Personal Memoirs | BIOGRAPHY & AUTOBIOGRAPHY / Medical | SELF-HELP / Post-Traumatic Stress Disorder (PTSD)
Classification: LCC R727.2 .G37 2021 | DDC 610.69/092--dc23

Cover Design and Interior Layout by Jesse Lundberg
Lundberg Graphics

Edited by Annie Jenkinson - Just Copyeditors
https://www.just-copyeditors.com

Dedication

This book is dedicated to all of you who
have experienced violence in your healthcare workplace.

And, to Jonathan Garen, MD, and Rachel Garen, MSW;
you are my gifts to the world.

May you always be safe.

Table of Contents

Introduction

Dear Friend,

While it may seem presumptuous to call you *friend*, I feel that we already started to build a relationship based on mutual regard when you picked up this book and decided to open it. I have been asked for whom this book is intended, and my response is that anyone who works in healthcare or is a consumer of healthcare services will have the opportunity to expand their perspective from the thoughts and stories it shares.

My goal is to help you understand the breadth and depth of violence in the healthcare workplace, while delivering ideas and resources to empower your healing. Statistics are important, but they're ever so impersonal. At the very least, I hope that this book will make you feel you have read deeply personal and insightful stories here, *not* numbers, and *not* statistics.

Other nurses who have survived workplace violence have honored me with the privilege of sharing their painful stories, and it is only because of all their sharing that I can say these narratives should serve to demonstrate the vast dimensions of violence as they pertain to healers—in every meaning of the word. By giving names and experiences to these otherwise anonymous statistical numbers, we can attach living souls to them.

Therefore, some of my book's key ingredients are the specific lessons learned while meandering along the post-assault healing journey, searching for my new place in the world, while other stories represent the other experiences of my colleagues in healthcare, the recollections they have so kindly shared with us all.

I can really only speak for myself in saying that I sincerely hope my shared journey offers you the opportunity to shift your thinking regarding healthcare workplace violence. All I ask is that you keep an open mind and an empathetic heart while reading.

Let me also say this in no uncertain terms, that the *healthcare field is a violent environment.* If you are thinking of a career in a healthcare work setting, you need to know this before you embark on your employment.

I say this not to deter you but to assist you. Healthcare, in all its many facets, offers a plethora of wonderful vocations, but being forewarned about inherent threats and challenges is always a big help in any role!

So, it's a simple statement, and I'll make no apologies for repeating it:

The healthcare field is a violent environment.

Consider it. Discuss it. Know it. Challenge it. Don't hide it or shy away from that fact.

But even as I say this, I am betting that as you read it, your first response may be to argue the validity of it. I can almost hear the statements:

"I know lots of nurses and nobody has ever mentioned this."
"I doubt it's quite this bad..."
"If someone is having this much of a problem with workplace violence, maybe it's more about them."

Please, before you push back and slam the cover shut, just stop for a minute, and think about it. Healthcare workers are physically and verbally assaulted by patients and visitors daily. Don't believe it? Ask them. That's all. Just *ask*. The fact they have never mentioned it to you or in general conversation may mean they are simply skating over the matter as so many of us have been taught to do, and as is expected to some degree. Perhaps, they have just given up. Ask them.

Within the hallowed halls of healing, lateral and vertical violence between the healthcare workers is routinely experienced at every level.

What a horrid conundrum to find yourself the victim of violence in an environment dedicated to healing. As a matter of fact, you have been tasked to "do no harm" while helping patients and their families to heal. Even more difficult to understand, then, is the notion of feeling entitled to perpetrate the victimization through violence of colleagues working in healthcare. As is so often the case in violence and abuse, it only becomes self-perpetuating from generation to generation, with the abused becoming the abusers.

Thus, complicity and a distinct lack of awareness have combined with the ever-increasing productivity pressures in the healthcare industry, allowing this malignancy of violence to grow undeterred.

Violence has extended its poisonous tentacles throughout the healthcare culture, in fact, resulting in it seemingly becoming ignored and/or supported by many who refuse to see it for what it is. The title of my book, in fact, says it all.

"Hey, I could use a little help here," is an expression I have heard used in a multitude of circumstances during my time in nursing, yet most commonly, it's used in reference to a challenging patient care situation. This phrase is loosely translated to "another set of hands is needed NOW to manage this hellish mess that I'm struggling, by myself, to turn around." While they seem benign, these simple words are meant to communicate a sense of urgency without alarming those on the periphery.

Crafting these words into the title of this book seemed only right to me. It seemed fitting. It is long past the time for healthcare workers to reframe the focus of this plea. We need to start utilizing these words to ask for and receive support navigating the troubled waters of healing our own wounds caused by healthcare workplace violence. We must begin working together to build an environment that supports healing, not only for those whom we are duty bound to provide care, but also for those delivering the care.

Mine is just one story of personal struggles and growth, definitely not a "one-size-fits-all" manual. I am only sharing what I have learned through trial and error. Remember, this isn't meant to be a research paper, but a narrative. If you want facts and figures, there are plenty around, and I will leave it to you to search for what you feel you need.

My hope is that by sharing my story, along with the continuing adventure to gain some sense of equilibrium, those of you who have also survived violence won't feel quite so alone on your journey. A community of survivors is a brave place to start the healing process, and sadly, for many, that community is difficult, if not impossible, to find.

I have spent my entire career at the bedside, where patients have been the stars around which my career has circled. ID badges have almost always included my title as "clinical nurse" or "staff nurse." I am therefore the first to say that my life has been relatively average, remarkably so. What I do have—in place of being a 'learned expert' with a bunch of high-level academic qualifications to talk about the subject of healthcare workplace violence—is the story born of an education gained while working in the trenches. I've seen a lot and done a lot. There is little that shocks me at this stage of the game.

While long lists of letters at the end of a name provide a sense of credibility for certain readers, I would offer that the same holds true for those who have survived a career spent in the foxholes of healthcare. No academic degrees can prepare you for a life in the trenches either, not even if you accrue several of them across several subjects.

I grew up in a small town in New England, never got into any impressive sort of trouble, graduated from college and nursing school, was married, had two amazing kids, got divorced, cared for my parents in their later years, and always worked hard to make a living and care for my family.

The majority of my nursing experience was then spent in the operating room, but after more than three decades of perioperative nursing, I became aware of an increasing disconnection between my professional values and those of the healthcare industry. The patients, it appeared, were only getting further away from me and healthcare was becoming more like a factory production line, with difficult or unachievable targets and a mass of paperwork.

When my last child was almost out of college, the moment had arrived to make a break for it and change my area of nursing practice.

I was hopeful that this would be the opportunity to truly make a difference in patients' lives–to return to what had made me want to be a nurse in the first place. After a fair amount of soul searching, I decided to accept a position as a clinical nurse in a psychiatric hospital, a position that would not only allow me the time to finish a graduate degree in nursing in the psychiatric mental health nurse practitioner program, but that would also offer me the opportunity to blend nursing with some of my original passion for social work. This career transition would become, without me knowing it, the impetus for sharing my journey of healing from healthcare workplace violence with you.

As we all know, many times in life, our personal agendas and the plans of the universe wind up taking remarkably divergent paths. Well, the detour I encountered was, without a doubt, wildly off my intended trajectory!

One evening, a few months after I had completed orientation at the psychiatric hospital, my world was tipped on its axis and, at this juncture, I became a number in the statistical data bank for healthcare workplace violence – if only that data had been collected at my workplace. Now, via that one incident, a complicated and often cruelly challenging world had just become the new normal for me.

As time has gone on, I have learned that what I lived through after the assault was not unique to me. For many of my colleagues, what I experienced was simply the industry standard for how employees injured in workplace violence are routinely treated. Many of you have walked or are walking similar paths, I know.

One story about healthcare workplace violence has especially tugged at my heartstrings. This particular narrative involved a nurse by the name of Lynne Truxillo. Her experience, in all of its horror and needless tragedy, became a catalyst for change in my own life. Her death sparked a fire in me that resulted in speaking out about healthcare workplace violence. Sadly, I never had the opportunity to meet Lynne in person. I am endlessly grateful, though, for the impact that she has had on my life and healing. Without her, I would not have found my voice nor would this book have been written.

The format of this book is unique. I have spent much of my career mentoring and orienting staff and students. Surprisingly for some, I really loved that part of my job. And I mean LOVED! Writing a book, on the other hand, is solitary work and I do miss interacting with colleagues. So, to make this experience more engaging for the reader, I arrived at the notion of incorporating bullet journal prompts in a few chapters.

Bullet journals are great because they don't require lengthy compositions, yet they offer a designated space for writing down clarifying thoughts and ideas about a topic. Plus, they feel a bit like a list; there are very few working in healthcare who don't utilize lists and checklists! Therefore, I am hopeful that you find it fun—and, perhaps, even a bit thought-provoking. Bust out your colored pencils, gel pens, crayons, and stickers. Feel free to run wild with this. Make the journal entries truly your own by being authentic with yourself.

The first step of growth and healing comes from taking an honest look at an uncomfortable situation and sitting in it for a bit. The journal prompts are meant to give you a safe space to do just that.

I caution against getting ahead of yourself as you engage in the journaling. Give yourself permission to marinate a bit when working on your entries. Don't feel that you must rush into action.

When taking this first step, please be compassionate with yourself and silence any harsh voice of self-judgment that may try to shame or criticize while you journal. Also, own your past actions without working to justify those that may now feel unjust to you. Learn to offer self-compassion and forgive yourself, using the activities and exercises as you wish, and trusting yourself implicitly to know what feels right for you. I understand that not everything resonates with everybody.

I am writing this on the eve of the third anniversary of being assaulted. Each year, as this date approaches, I notice the way the air feels and smells, a sensory input that invariably takes me right back to the day of the assault. This season, while taxing for me, is also a clear reminder that healing is a journey.

A part of me continues to grieve what has been lost along with what, now, will never be. Three years ago, I worked my last shift as a nurse, and just like that, a career had ended. Funny how something so central to my existence and identity for so long could be taken away from me without consideration or warning, so quickly, almost in the blink of an eye.

This book may be the final place where you will find me identified by RN, the professional title I have proudly been using for over three decades. Grief has eventually begun to give way to a small glimmer of acceptance of my feelings of loss of this integral part of my identity. By learning to relinquish my attachment to what no longer identifies me, the door opens to new and different opportunities to use many of the skills that I took for granted while working in nursing.

And, so, my journey continues.

This book is the product of the lessons that I have painstakingly learned on this pathway of recovery, but in writing it, I've learned an important lesson that perhaps I had never understood before. This is the lesson that *being assaulted at work does not define me*; being a *survivor* of that assault does, at least to some degree. The assault and my survival do undeniably have a major bearing on who I am now, on who I needed to become after I had escaped it and recovered from it.

I would never wish my experience on anyone, but can finally appreciate it for the challenges and opportunities with which it has provided me. All that has gone on before has contributed to making me who I am today, and it is my privilege and honor to share those insights and exercises with you.

Your own story of experiencing workplace violence is important. Your thoughts, ideas, and feelings about this pervasive issue in healthcare have enormous value. I don't know what path brought you to open this book, but I am very glad that you are here.

I earnestly hope that you will find the contents of this book helpful while navigating the extremely choppy and hazardous waters of healthcare workplace violence. Please know that you aren't alone.

It's okay if you need to call out for a little help here.

June Zanes Garen, RN

Bullet Journal #1

Three words that I use to describe myself are:

-
-
-

Now, just for fun, draw something that you feel symbolizes one of your unique qualities:

Please don't overthink this one. What are three strengths upon which you rely in your daily adventures?

-
-
-

Chapter 1:

Lynne Sausse Truxillo, RN

~

October 13, 1962 ~ April 11, 2019

This chapter is dedicated to the memory of Lynne Sausse Truxillo, RN, who died on April 11, 2019 from injuries sustained during a patient assault while on duty at Baton Rouge General Hospital.

While my family was engaging in wedding festivities and embracing all that New Orleans had to offer, another family nearby was heading off to a very different kind of life event.

It is not my place to intrude on the privacy of people collecting the pieces of their lives, which have been shattered by the loss of a loved one. As I pen this chapter, I am mindful that it has been barely a year since the life of a mother, daughter, sister, wife, aunt, friend, and colleague was tragically taken from the world.

A year is such a short time, no doubt measured doggedly in holidays, family gatherings, life celebrations, and seasons. I can only imagine how each of these hurdles lays open the scars of that loss. Please understand, I am writing solely from my own heart with information supplemented by a simple internet search of Lynne Truxillo, RN.

Before I tell you Lynne's story, let me explain that in the year between finishing a degree in social work and starting nursing school, I worked in a nursing home. Often, our elderly patients were mere shadows of the people they had been during the more robust periods of their lives. While working there, I began reading obituaries in a much more probing manner. After all, an obituary could be deemed the final summary and a statement of the life lived, and reading those residents' final stories pushed my thinking about the foundations of what would end up being truly important in life. An obituary served—and serves—the vital purpose of boiling down the sap of living into the sweet syrup of remembrance.

Much of what we think is vitally essential to attain and maintain a good life—filled with well-organized financial stability and a svelte physique—is boiled away. The essential ingredients of an eternal legacy—family, friends, compassion, traditions, and integrity—provide the pleasant taste that lingers. From reading Lynne's obituary, I have learned that Lynne left many footprints on the journey of her life. Her abundant legacy contains the sweetness of humor, loyalty, kindness, love, and the gift of providing a healing touch for those who were struggling.

I do not want this discussion to be defined by speaking about the person who assaulted Lynne, so this is in no way meant to be construed as being his story. The back story is important though, to appreciate the terrifying road that Lynne was forced to travel. My focus is on *who she was and what we have lost*.

This story began on April 4, 2019, when a patient initiated an altercation with one of Lynne's fellow nurses. Lynne stepped in to protect her colleague and the patient subsequently turned his attention to physically assaulting her. During that violent attack, Lynne sustained multiple injuries, which, according to the medical examiner, ultimately cost her life. In medical speak, Lynne experienced pulmonary emboli (blood clots in blood vessels going to the lung) which caused her condition to deteriorate and require cardiopulmonary resuscitation. The resuscitation attempt failed. Lynne was gone and a family was plunged into loss and grief.

Monday morning quarterbacking has no place here. We don't get to dissect Lynne's response to the assault on her co-worker. You and I were not there. All of our hypotheses of what we would have done if we had been in Lynne's place are irrelevant and only provide us with the opportunity to open the door to useless judgments and criticism. We weren't there. We may think that we know what our response would be in a similar experience, but until we are tested as Lynne was, I contend that none of us truly knows what we would do in the situation she faced on that April day.

At this point, you may even be wondering why I feel compelled to spend time ruminating on the life and times of a woman I have never met. From what I have read about Lynne Truxillo, however, I know that I would have liked her. According to the articles written, she was fun, and funny, a devoted mother, and she received an award for being an exemplary volunteer at her children's school. She was passionate about helping people and loved nursing.

She hailed from New Orleans and loved all things Mardi Gras.

What gave me a strong sense of kinship and fierceness about a stranger's death? Quite simply, as I looked at the list of her injuries sustained in a patient assault, I understood that it could have been written about me.

I was spared; Lynne wasn't. It was that simple.

It became even clearer when I considered all the pivotal events Lynne and her family had missed. My daughter was chosen to fill the role of "best man," or as she preferred to call it, "best buddy" at her brother's wedding, and I was the one who accompanied her to pick out the dress for the big day.

I saw my son get married and would soon be watching him graduate from medical school. Small things. Or are they? To a grieving family, these are momentous events that have been robbed of a chance to be thoroughly, completely, happy ones. An empty space has taken the place of the one who should have been there, but has been abruptly snatched away.

Lynne was robbed of those sorts of events. While I have a voice, Lynne's was forcibly taken from her. In dying, Lynne gave me something which had been missing since I was attacked – a clarity of purpose. As she rushed in to help a co-worker, she provided an example to all of us. Lynne's story helped me to find my own voice to advocate for safe healthcare workplaces, and to share ideas and resources for healing from violence experienced within that workplace.

I can imagine the horror of watching a colleague being attacked. I worry about the coworker who Lynne protected that day, since being a survivor can be so bittersweet. I can feel the shock of how quickly the violence escalated, tasting the bitterness from the desperation of being so alone in the immediate first seconds of the downwardly spiraling situation.

I can breathe the "canned" hospital air and smell the anguish of not knowing how this whole mess will finally play out.

I can picture Lynne stepping in without hesitation to protect a co-worker. She probably did not even think about it. She just did it.

I can sense the urgency and potential doom preceding Lynne's final trip to the hospital, and can sense the fear of defeat on April 11, 2019, as the medical staff at the hospital where Lynne died realized that the resuscitation attempts were unsuccessful.

What a difficult pill this must have been to swallow when they had to "call the code" and state the time of death for one of their own.

Even now, writing this, I am weighed down by the shock and heaviness in my chest at the thought of Lynne's family, waiting nervously for news of a wife and mother, having to be told that she has died.

We all lost so much that day, but Lynne's family suffered the most tremendous loss of all. The story is Lynne's and theirs. It is not mine; I can only feel and imagine the ripples in the pool of their lives, after that stone was brutally thrown into it. I can only imagine their pain and suffering. But I feel that we all must try to understand; we all must let Lynne and others like Lynne live on by not letting her death be in vain.

Lynne, you see, filled an ample space in the universe, yet her family now faces a world where an enormous void has taken her place. Her seat will remain empty on holidays and at family dinners. Her images will be missing from her children's wedding photos. Her lap won't be there for future grandbabies. Her head won't be on the pillow next to her husband's at night, and no longer will Lynne rise to make him a cup of coffee in the morning, or to ask him how his day was, or to hand him the remote control for the television. The small things are missed just the same as the big things. Lynne's family has to suffer them all.

The rest of us have lost a kind, compassionate, and selfless healer. Our humanity has been diminished.

I'd like to think that there is a heaven with a spot reserved in it for people who work in healthcare. I can almost picture how lovely it would be… full of color, flowers, and lots of sparkles.

I envision this beautiful nurse greeting newcomers by organizing the resident souls into one of the traditional New Orleans events, a Second Line. I close my eyes and see a long parade full of departed friends, family, and colleagues waving handkerchiefs and dancing happily behind a celestial brass jazz band playing that old Big Easy classic, "When the Saints Go Marching in."

Rest in peace, Lynne.

Chapter 2:

A Little Historical Perspective

Decades ago, I learned that much could be discovered if we would just take a moment to glance in the rearview mirror. We are blessed with the opportunity to see where we have been, where traps and snares have been hidden, and what has been helpful or a hindrance while managing the pathway previously walked.

Perhaps, most importantly, taking time for a backward glance gives some necessary perspective on what our next step could be to aid in moving forward with purpose, while also minimizing risk. Looking at history helps us be proactive rather than assuming the knee-jerk response of reactivity. Personally, I tend to discourage the reactive approach because it rarely ever seems to shine when we take stock of our actions retrospectively.

Not all of history is in books; much of what we can learn comes from people who lived through tough times. I clearly remember a story from my teenage years that exemplifies this sort of anecdotal wisdom.

My father worked the evening shift in a woodturning mill, while my mother, a nurse, worked the day shift at the local hospital. I attended a parochial high school located an hour away from the town where my parents worked.

I would get up in the wee hours to ride in with my mother before she started her shift, take a bus to school, participate in a full day of educational activities, ride the bus back to town, wait for Mom to get out of work to pick me up, ride home, and then get ready to do it all over again the next day. This story is my personal version of the classic "walking five miles uphill to and from school in a blizzard."

Sometimes, my father would arrive early and meet me at the bus stop. From there, we would head over to the library, settle on a bench by the war memorials, and have a little chinwag while I waited to go home. After I was collected, Dad would head off to start his shift at the mill.

I don't remember exactly how our conversation started this one particular afternoon, but it meandered along to finally discussing the names on the World War I memorial located near the bench where we were sitting. I read through to see how many were familiar. There were, seemingly, whole columns of people with the same last name. In the 1970's, there were still descendants of those memorialized living locally. This wasn't particularly surprising since folks were not as inclined to leave their birthplace as they are nowadays.

My father knew the majority of the families and had gone to school with many relatives of the people whose names were engraved on those bronze plaques. Most interesting to me were the names with stars next to them... those who had made the "ultimate sacrifice" and died in the war. I realized that there were even females with stars next to their names, how odd! There certainly weren't any women fighting in combat way back then, so how could these women have died in a war? My father explained that the majority of the women listed on the memorial were nurses who had died from the 1918 influenza pandemic.

And sure enough, as I am writing this, nurses and doctors are dying in yet another global pandemic: COVID-19. History repeats itself as we continue to lose dedicated healers.

My mother was from the Netherlands. She attended nurses' training at a Deaconess Hospital after the end of World War II, and her toe-curling stories of what she saw and did there struck terror in my heart. Her nursing student experience sounded a bit like being an indentured servant in a penal institution. There were few resources, human or material, left in the Netherlands after enduring five years of a hostile occupation during the war.

Mom told me stories about the patients she had cared for who, after being liberated from the death camps, returned to homes that no longer existed. These people were often broken in body and spirit, and the burden of the war years and their aftermath left a permanent mark on my mother. Her perspective on the value of life, dignity, respect, and death had a strong influence on my own nursing practice.

This little narrative may help illustrate the impact that surviving the war had on my mother's approach to life and death. Many years ago, our local hospital acquired equipment for transporting the bodies of patients who had died, taking them from the nursing ward to the hospital morgue. We have all seen these contraptions, consisting of a stretcher with a sort of covered flat tent frame which goes over the body, so that when loaded, it just looks like a very tall but empty stretcher; albeit it's a stretcher obviously pushing a large amount of 'dead' weight.

My mother was horrified. She thought that it was disgraceful and lacking in respect that anyone would even consider hiding a patient in such an undignified manner. In her mind, death was as much a part of life as birth. How could people stop and pay their solemn respects if her patient was being carted off and hidden away like a bag of unpleasant garbage? She maintained that her patient was still her patient through the important rituals around post-mortem care, and this relationship didn't end until the door of the morgue closed behind her after delivering that patient's body to the final destination.

The story about her maiden voyage using this contraption is worth hearing. Mom instructed the orderly accompanying her on the passage to the morgue to carry the ungainly top piece of the equipment. He was to walk behind her while she pushed her patient, freshly bathed and in a clean johnny, who was completely covered with a clean sheet. Patients and visitors stopped, lips moved with silent prayers, rosary beads were quickly produced, heads were bowed, a death was acknowledged, and then, life resumed. She felt that she had completed her final bit of nursing care with dignity and respect. No big surprise that Mom also taught me that if we don't agree with something, we must speak up. Silence means complicity, and given my mother's experience during WWII, she had learned that complicity opened the door to allow hideous outcomes.

Nurses have been around since we began walking upright. As anyone who has taken an introductory nursing class has learned, we have a rich and interesting history. Historical perspective gives us a sense of our roots and heritage. Sometimes, it also helps us to understand and retain important pieces of our cultural identity to grasp tightly as we move into the future.

So, bear with me for a little refresher. Please be aware that this version may sound a bit different than the beginning chapters of any Nursing 101 texts; this is entirely written from my own somewhat meandering viewpoint.

Healers and nurturers existed long before they were called nurses. The term "deaconess" can be traced to women performing nursing duties in homes as far back as early Christian times. There was a strong connection between the budding Christian Church and caring for the sick. The first hospital, though, didn't come into existence until after 650 AD and, by today's standards, it was a primitive setup with patients arranged around the altar in a convent chapel in Beaune, France. While there was no formal training for the nurses, compassion and religious devotion provided a basis for caring.

England provides the scene for the historical stories we have all heard and loved. After the Protestant Reformation ended (1648), the land and buildings owned by the Catholics were all seized. The religious hospitals were gone, so, in their absence, the sick without families were stored in almshouses and public hospitals. These institutions were neither treatment nor outcome-oriented; they were effectively just human warehouses in which disreputable women (prostitutes, drunkards, thieves, and all manner of unsavory sorts) were forced to be caregivers.

While it does seem more than a little titillating to consider these lascivious, drinking, brawling, thieving criminal types as the foundation of modern nursing, that wasn't really the case. They were just forced to fill the gap until the real mother of modern nursing, Florence Nightingale, arrived on the scene.

Florence was clever and resourceful. She came from money

and had a solid classical education, as well as having received a formal nursing education at a Deaconess House in Germany. Florence was also committed to public health, keeping meticulous records and managing statistics about patient treatments and outcomes. I would also say that, in my mind, Florence Nightingale had an evidence-based practice well before that idea even existed. She headed off to the Crimean War, cleaned up a filthy military field hospital, gave the patients basic nursing care, and documented that the survival rate dramatically improved—evidence, indeed, that squalor and filth would not promote health. She was also savvy at navigating politics to get what her patients needed. While we see her looking quite angelic with a lamp in her hand, I think that she was actually a committed social activist who was not afraid to speak up on behalf of those who couldn't speak for themselves. She was a fearless patient advocate regarding everything she knew to be right and fair. In today's language, I think that Florence would probably be considered a badass.

Legend has it that Florence Nightingale was nicknamed Lady with a Hammer by some of the physicians and military officers; perhaps they meant this moniker as an insult, since it described Florence in most unladylike terms. Apparently, if the people in charge refused to unlock closets so that she could access supplies needed for her patients, Florence would take matters into her own hands by using a hammer to open the door. Florence Nightingale went on to establish the Nightingale School of Nursing in London. She is definitely one of my heroes.

The evolution of nursing in America was shaped a little differently. The melting pot of cultures, combined with the vast geographic contours of the land, added unique dimensions and challenges.

Before the Revolutionary War, when the colonies had pockets of settlers from other countries, some small hospitals were established by religious orders. The French settled in New Orleans in 1699. As time went on, it became apparent to the local government officials that there was a lack of adequate nursing care for the locals.

As the result of a great deal of political and religious negotiations, it was arranged that a group of Ursuline nuns would go to the New World to work as teachers and nurses. After a grueling journey by ship from France, sixteen nuns arrived in New Orleans in 1727.

Not surprisingly, they found the conditions more miserable than their grimmest expectations, yet they still tackled their missions with vigor and diligence. If you ever get to New Orleans, I would certainly encourage you to take a tour around the Ursuline Convent on Chartres Street. This building not only housed the nuns, but it also provided space for a school and hospital. Oh, to assume the proverbial 'fly on the wall' spot back in the 1700's to see what life was like!

During the Revolutionary War, George Washington realized that in order to maintain the health and fighting readiness of the Continental Army, it was necessary to incorporate nurses into his request for support from the Continental Congress. He also required that matrons be utilized to supervise the quality and economy of care delivered to the soldiers. I find it fascinating that even the father of our country made sure that the most exact economy was observed. See, history *does* keep repeating itself.

Not long after Florence was busy opening closets with her hammer in the Crimea, nursing care began to evolve in America. Prior to the Civil War, much of the care required by the sick or injured had been provided in the home by women. These women based much of their delivery of care on wisdom handed down through generations, and, I'm guessing, on exciting runs of trial and error.

Doctors made house calls to diagnose and direct. Hospitals were established in larger cities, but most of the country was still quite rural. In the South, the responsibilities of nursing the sick and injured fell on the shoulders of female slaves.

The Civil War saw a desperate need for nurses to care for the wounded soldiers. Elizabeth Blackwell, the first female physician trained in the United States, had the foresight to develop a training course to prepare nurses to care for Yankee soldiers wounded on the battlefields of the Civil War. Clara Barton, the founder of the Red Cross, and Dorothea Dix were also key figures organizing and delivering care during this tragic period.

I would be remiss not to bring up an important pioneer in nursing, Mary Eliza Mahoney (1845-1926), the first trained African American nurse. Back in the early 1980's when I was in nursing school, Mary Mahoney was not a staple of our history of nursing textbooks. I am hopeful that now, we respectfully acknowledge her for not only being a brilliant nurse, social activist, and nurse advocate, but also for her astonishing achievements in breaking down racial barriers to gain access to nursing education.

An interesting side note: Mary Mahoney was a dedicated suffragette. She was one of the first women to register to vote in Boston, MA. Search for her name on the Internet; I think that you will find her achievements both humbling and inspiring.

Times were changing in the U.S. and the population was growing.

Cities were becoming urban centers. Medical schools were established. Building hospitals became a priority in order to provide a pool of patients for the education of medical students. As patients began receiving more centralized care in hospitals, the growth of hospital-based training for nurses quickly followed suit.

Nursing now turned its attention to the working poor and immigrant populations surviving in the rough, dirty urban areas. I learned of the settlement house movement both in social work courses as well as in nursing classes. Jane Addams, another hero of mine, worked unceasingly to promote health and education for the growing immigrant population. Jane Addams was the first American woman to receive a Nobel Peace Prize. She also established a formal school of social work.

The settlement house philosophy moved in a new direction to assist the poor and struggling. Charity was replaced with empowerment. This shift was demonstrated through advocating for better conditions, improved education, and the provision of healthcare for the underserved. Many of the roots of modern social work, health promotion, and public health nursing are found in this movement.

Wars have also had an enormous impact on the need and subsequent growth of the nursing profession. Nurses continued to accompany soldiers to the battlefield with each conflict bringing about changes and challenges in the delivery of care.

As a new Operating Room (OR) nurse, I remember talking with a surgeon who had gone to Vietnam straight out of his surgical residency. We spoke about all of the medical advances that had come from the different wars. Those discoveries and improvements became life-changing blessings that eventually filtered out to the general population. The advanced technology and improved medical techniques always challenged nurses to prepare to care for more serious injuries and illnesses with the goal of decreasing mortality rates and improving quality of life.

WWII brought about increased survival rates with the availability of antibiotics, while the Korean War shaped the practice of vascular surgery and allowed many soldiers to go home without losing limbs that would have been amputated in earlier conflicts.

The Vietnam War influenced the outcome of trauma patients by providing fast transportation for medical interventions. In my more recent memory—long-term conflict in the Middle East has fueled the study of traumatic brain injury and complex prosthetics for patients with combat injuries requiring the amputation of limbs closer to the torso, in which only a comparatively shorter stump is available for the attachment of prostheses.

Nursing has not only had to keep in step with technical advances, but it has also had major shifts within its own culture. The nurses' training that my mother endured in the 1940's no longer exists. Mom worked like a skivvy during the first few years of nursing school, since it was expected that students would provide, for free, elbow grease to keep the institution running. Indeed, in her early days at the Diakonessenhuis in Hilversum, Netherlands, there were strict schedules complete with vigorously enforced curfews. When I heard her stories of nursing school, I thought that it sounded like a dreadful hybrid between a correctional facility and military basic training. There was definitely some fun to be had, though. Mom remained lifelong friends with her nursing school roommate, Jetty. When they met up much later for a visit, Mom and Jetty laughed about their nursing school shenanigans. As a young girl, I loved hearing them howl over the stories of Jetty's romantic adventures. These escapades often kept Jetty out past the regulation curfew. The solution to getting back into the building after the door was locked involved an exciting combination of physical prowess, daring antics, and an accomplice. Jetty would make her way up to the window of their room on the second floor by way of a tree, while my mother, her loyal accomplice, would be waiting on the inside to open the window and pull Jetty in to safety. Crazy, right?

Nurses are now educated in colleges and universities, and a Bachelor of Science in Nursing (BSN) is the entry-level educational requirement for many nursing positions. It is not uncommon, however, for some in the profession to aspire to more advanced degrees.

The old-school student nurses' quarters and caps have gone the way of hoop skirts. The educational undercurrent has also changed; and when I was in nursing school, it was emphasized that nurses were educated, not trained. Circus animals would be trained, not healthcare professionals.

As I currently read this narrative of my profession, I see a common thread that still holds firm today. Simply, throughout history, nurses have stepped up when they are needed. Nurses have a long history of meeting challenges in often overwhelming situations. As I said earlier, history does repeat itself.

Bullet Journal #2

Give yourself time to think about who has inspired you in your chosen profession. What did they do to encourage you to move forward with any challenges you may have faced?

-
-
-

Are you inspired by somebody in history? What is it about them that resonates with you? Jot down the words that you think describe the attributes that you share with your historical hero.

-
-
-

What words do you hope will be used to describe you to future generations?

-
-
-

People, whether famous, infamous, close acquaintances, or someone we have never met, shape our ideas, beliefs, and attitudes. Who has helped to mold you into the person you are? Describe this person.

My historical heroes (famous or not) are:

•

•

•

Role models don't have to be the "whole package." Sometimes, people display one particular trait that you really admire. Who are some of your role models? What traits do they possess that you would most like to incorporate into your own life?

•

•

•

Chapter 3:

*DJ**

"I feel that if I help one kid, I've done what I was put there to do."

I spoke with DJ for over an hour on a cold, rainy Sunday afternoon. She had just finished her week of twelve-hour night shifts on an adolescent behavioral health unit. Her passion for and love of being a nurse was apparent from the very start of our conversation.

DJ spoke of her background and the foundation she had gained from her strong, supportive family. Her mother was a nurses' aide and her father an orderly at the local hospital. DJ remembers them working opposite shifts so that she and her siblings always had one parent at home. She spoke lovingly of family dinners, going to church on Sundays, and always feeling safe and supported while she was growing up. I asked what had inspired her to pursue a career in nursing. Without hesitation, she offered that it had just seemed a natural choice, given the atmosphere in which she had been raised.

It takes very little imagination to envision how challenging it is to work the night shift, or any shift, on an adolescent psych unit. Young, physically healthy yet emotionally broken, souls come with a myriad of struggles that serve to amplify the run-of-the-mill challenges facing adolescents today.

Sometimes, this toxic and overwhelming mix creates an inability to forge ahead in the world and intervention becomes necessary. Behavioral issues and mental health diagnoses are precarious ledges from which a misstep can result in life-changing outcomes not only for the patients, but also for those around them.

Now bear in mind, nursing is a second career for DJ.

Previously, she had worked with children in a daycare setting and in human services. Becoming a nurse had been her dream. She fulfilled it by finishing her education in the evenings while working and raising her family; it was her determination that got her through the nine years that it took to complete her education and become a registered nurse.

As she put it, "I wanted the fairy tale nursing job… to take care of babies."

Unfortunately, those jobs were in short supply for a recent graduate, and DJ needed employment to support her family. Then, she spotted a position at a local psychiatric facility; fortuitously, they were looking for a nurse on their adolescent unit. She applied and received the magical call for an interview the next day. DJ saw this as a sign that this position was quite possibly, "What I'm supposed to be doing." The cynics among us might have offered to DJ that it was more likely a sign of desperation on the part of the employer.

Life is an ever-changing and challenging stockpot of experiences and, in fairness, I need to step back for a moment and set the stage for those nine years that DJ spent in nursing school.

She was open about sharing her family's health struggles and about the imprint that it left on her personally and professionally. DJ's first husband was diagnosed with paranoid schizophrenia. Not having a partner with whom to share responsibilities is often a struggle in itself; trying to cope with the addition of a psychiatric illness and its resulting chaos would be impossible for many. Yet, DJ persevered and succeeded, despite having the odds stacked against her. She not only finished her nursing program, but also continued to nurture her children.

DJ is both compassionate and caring; she is quick to throw in a generous dollop of encouragement for her young patients. She has walked a path similar to theirs and understands the situation; she can speak honestly from a position of having survived the journey.

I was intrigued by the strength of DJ's conviction about her work. I had to ask what fueled the passion I was hearing in her voice about her nursing practice and her patients.

The answer was simple: DJ has infinite compassion for her young patients who are struggling with life. Often, these kids face obstacles that seem insurmountable. She spoke with love and kindness about her patients who are admitted with suicide attempts, depression, anxiety, or for substance misuse. I heard her strength when she talked about the privilege of witnessing their feelings of desperation and supporting them in healing. DJ has remained in this nursing position for over ten years.

I asked DJ what her experience has been with violence at work. She succinctly explained that she has noted a gradual shift in the underpinnings of the client base combined with dwindling organizational support for the culture of care. The calling, which she not so long ago had loved, has now moved into more of a love/hate relationship.

Over the span of ten years, the physical design of the hospital unit has been changed to an "open" concept to make it feel less institutional and more welcoming for the patients. This means that there is no longer a place to go where the staff can safely get away from aggressive patients.

The industry goal of managing the financial bottom line rules the admission process. This goal results in a constant push to keep every bed filled, regardless of patient acuity or aggression. Staff members are often put on the spot to justify why a violent patient requires a single room because of safety concerns.

DJ noted that she had also seen a change in the patient profile admitted to the unit. There seems to be a trend more related to unmanageable behavior rather than diagnosed mental illness. These new patients often come through the door of the hospital after acting out in a violent episode at home. Police presence is required when the family can no longer cope with the unsafe behaviors — and this police intervention often results in the patient being admitted to an already over-stretched hospital where the violent behavior continues.

It is sort of an inverse ratio, it appears... violent patients on the rise, while institutional safety mechanisms are ever-diminishing. What has this been like for DJ?

When I spoke with DJ, she offered that she has a feeling of defeat before she even clocks in for her shift. She said that her time at work is routinely spent dealing with outrage, violence, and outbursts.

She simply stated, "I go from fire to fire to fire." All the while, she finds herself defending clinical judgment and medical decisions regarding whether or not it is safe for another patient to be admitted to the unit. The institutional goal of keeping the beds full and revenue rolling in must always be considered.

So, where does this kind of scenario leave the nurse's ethical mandate to "do no harm?" Increasingly, nursing staff see how this simply runs headlong into a battle with balancing the budget. It just isn't possible for healers like DJ to feel as though they are meeting the mandate to do no harm if they are repeatedly pushed into making decisions that are heavily weighted in favor of the budget rather than the needs of the already strained patient care unit.

The upshot is that it isn't always possible to do what is safe for both the staff and patients under the pressure of relentless and unyielding financial targets.

Healers bring more to the table than just their credentials and education; they bring themselves. I asked how DJ was feeling now about her calling to work in this arena. The drop in her energy level was palpable as she answered. She said she had witnessed its negative impact, not only on herself, but also on her loved ones.

Not too long ago, DJ remarried.

DJ related to me that as a couple, they now find that the workplace violence from her job sits at the dinner table like an unwelcome guest between them; they might as well set the table for three.

DJ's husband struggles to listen to the rundown of how her shift went. Once a Marine, always a Marine... Semper Fi. He is hard-wired from his experience in the U.S. Marine Corps to protect, serve, and function as a cohesive team. After spending time in the military, violence is not a stranger to him. The senseless violence directed toward the nursing staff in the workplace, often at the woman he loves, frustrates him.

He finds the idea that she is supposed to prevent aggression without any tools or technology is contrary to logic. In preparation for the heat of battle, he learned to trust and depend on his leaders as integral pieces of the team; in his experience, leaders watch out for the safety of those for whom they are responsible. The leadership culture of abandoning the staff trying to manage the episodes of violence without back up or resources is baffling to him. There doesn't seem to be anybody in "leadership" actually watching out for the foot soldiers holding the line. Simply put, it just isn't right to him, and there is no justification that holds water.

DJ's grandchildren are mystified by the bruises that she sports as symbols of a really bad night at work. They cannot begin to understand why someone would hurt the grandmother they adore. DJ admits that she is unable to sleep the night before her work week starts, always finding herself anxious and more than a little nauseated. She muses, a little sadly, that she may actually be starting to hate her job.

Most nights, she feels a soul-sucking sense of defeat before even going through the hospital door because, while using the majority of her time and energy to extinguish those violent fires, there are still the non-violent kids who are admitted during acute mental health crises. These broken souls need her help. Little time and scant resources are left for them after all of the firefighting.

Perhaps, most telling, is the sadness in DJ's voice when I ask about the support she receives from management. The prevailing philosophy is one of holding the frontline staff responsible for violent episodes that come to the administration's attention. The first question asked of staff is, "What could you have done differently to have prevented this from happening?"

This question immediately deflects the accountability for securing a safe workplace away from the very people who hold the power to ensure it for both patients and staff. The message sent to the frontline staff is one of shame and blame. Support for the witnesses of violence and those injured is oftentimes lacking. The frontline staff members find that maintaining a defensive position is tiresome and physically wearing... especially when the offensive players are far more numerous and powerful.

Providing nursing care in this environment is beyond difficult.

Safety is a very basic human need. When that need is left unmet, it can be difficult to succeed or excel in accomplishing more diverse goals. I admire DJ for continuing to plod on in spite of the physical, emotional, and spiritual drain. After all, as she said, "I feel that if I help one kid, I've done what I was put there to do."

***

ADDENDUM: A few months after our interview, DJ left the nursing position described in the interview.

She had finally moved on after spending eleven years working in the foxholes of inpatient adolescent psychiatry. DJ made this change to save one more life... this time, her own. Due to concerns regarding the increasingly negative impact of the job on her physical health, DJ made the decision to move to a new practice area. She continues to work in nursing and has accepted a position that does not require any direct patient contact.

*Name changed at interviewee's request for anonymity.

Chapter 4:

I Think That the Tree is Dying

Geologically speaking, I have spent but a minute fraction of a millisecond working as a nurse. Looking back on my three-plus decades in nursing, however, the impact and number of changes I have experienced is quite impressive.

Once again, I am writing this from a personal viewpoint. We are all different and have a multitude of life experiences. Diversity, when combined with respect, empathy, and compassion, makes the whole of us vibrant and strong.

When I was a new graduate, the majority of the nurses I worked with had been educated in diploma schools of nursing which were affiliated with hospitals. I came from a university-based two-year degree nursing program.

In the early 1980's, very few of my colleagues had Bachelor of Science in Nursing (BSN) after their names. When I graduated from the school of nursing, my diploma granted me an Associate's Degree in "technical nursing." The group of BSN graduates at the ceremony were given the same diploma, the only difference being that it was in "professional nursing." My first position after nursing school was in a hospital that still had its own diploma school of nursing. My experience there was an eye opener. While I felt a little odd sporting the title of "technical nurse" on graduation day, I was now thrown into a pool of folks who were suspicious of anyone who had received a college-based nursing education rather than hospital-based nurses' training. It was challenging to safely navigate this climate of educational divide.

Nursing education continues to be a source of angst, especially among the frontline members of the profession. The admission fee to advancement in the profession consists of acquiring more education; however, this is not only expensive, but it is also tricky to excel at when combined with the competing demands of work and family. Now, there is a trend by both professional nursing organizations and employers to mandate that nurses complete their BSN as an entry-level educational requirement, and some positions in nursing are not open to licensed, registered nurses with less than a BSN degree.

At the same time, with more people attempting to meet the educational requirements for a BSN, there are fewer nursing instructors available to teach them. The American Association of Colleges of Nursing (AACN), which exists as the national voice for academic nursing, issued a report not long ago on the 2018-2019 Enrollment and Graduations in Baccalaureate and Graduate Programs in Nursing. Alarmingly, the AACN reported that 75,029 qualified applicants were denied admission to baccalaureate and graduate nursing programs in 2018. The main reason for not accepting these applicants was the shortage of faculty to staff the nursing programs. Lack of financial resources, clinical preceptors and sites, and classroom space also contributed to turning away tens of thousands of people who wanted to either become nurses or further their education in nursing.

I have seen and felt the log jam caused by this conundrum. While employers may demand that the coursework to complete a degree must be accomplished within a limited time frame to maintain employment, there is no guarantee that there will be a spot available in a program or local facility willing to provide a spot for the required clinical internship.

Uniforms are the mark of certain professions; nursing is no different. I was grateful that the decision had been made to put nursing caps in mothballs by the time I arrived on the scene. Nursing school pins, white uniforms, and white duty shoes were still the order of the day, though. When I was a newly minted nurse, I even had to wear white stockings as part of the mandatory professional attire. Such a lot of white. Now, we see nurses sporting a wide variety of colors and footwear.

The state of the art has leaped ahead at a terrifying pace. For example, many healthcare workers now document in real time on a computer rather than the antiquated pen and paper method. Patients now may have the opportunity to access medical records and their physician online. Telemedicine has become a reality and isn't just a concept in science fiction movies.

Hepatitis B is prevented by a commonly administered vaccine. AIDS has become a chronic illness rather than an automatic death sentence; I had graduated from nursing school before it had even been named. Hepatitis C can be cured with a course of medications.

It also seems amazing to think that many surgical procedures that used to be accomplished by way of large open incisions are now performed with minimally invasive techniques requiring complex equipment and robots. For example, having your gallbladder removed used to necessitate a long hospital stay with weeks of recovery at home. Now, many patients are back in their own homes on the same day and back at work within a week of having a cholecystectomy.

Not all of the changes that I have witnessed have been positive advancements, however. Obesity—and its accompanying comorbidities—is on the uptick. Mental illness, and the lack of services available to help those struggling with it, is a problem across the country. Substance misuse with its devastating impact, both personally and societally, is occurring at levels of epic proportions. Gun violence has increased to the point that it is now recognized as a public health epidemic.

It is impossible to overlook one of the other major players in the healthcare game: politics. Unfortunately, we might also say that politics have become a scourge, too, overriding and overwhelming the science of medicine. Funding and regulations are seemingly driven by political parties and lobbies with little or no vision of the ultimate impact on the lives of patients or healers. Budgets are key and healthcare is a privilege not afforded to all. Thus, health disparity is ever widening as many find access to care difficult to navigate and obtain. From my perspective, the view at the frontline is quite different than that in the boardroom or debate floor. In the trenches, we see faces, frustration, suffering, and waiting rooms packed to capacity; not a balance sheet, profit margin or political platform.

Some of the seemingly marvelous advancements in technology have been shown to hurt, rather than help, the patients. Just think for a moment about the ads that you have seen on highway billboards for personal injury and medical malpractice lawyers. I have observed several of these beacons offering legal resolutions and restitution for injuries from products that were, at one time, cutting-edge miracles promising to drastically improve lives. Sadly, however, they merely ended up in a deleterious nose dive into the pool of catastrophic outcomes, taking injured patients with them.

Let's not pretend that medicine and healthcare do not operate as businesses; they are businesses, through and through. Bottom lines, numbers, and productivity drive many of the decisions made today regarding the healthcare that we deliver and access as consumers.

The biggest, most concerning shift in healthcare and nursing relates to how we view it today. I remember hearing repeatedly that nursing is a combination of art and science. It feels as though we have moved far away from this notion in recent years. Healthcare has become a multi-billion-dollar industry and, as such, I have witnessed a dramatic disconnect between the cultural values relied upon for sustainability of the medical and nursing professions and the overpowering current business climate of an industry.

It was an expectation at my first position in the operating room that, as soon as the patient arrived in the room, he or she became the center of the staff's universe. Other tasks needed to be organized either before the patient arrived or after they were positioned for the start of the procedure.

Every patient's hand was held as they lost consciousness during the anesthesia induction. All of the staff had to be focused on the patient. All of the professionals in the room meshed together as a team sharing this common goal.

Fast forward a few decades to my last interview for an OR position.

The interviewer shared the necessity for increased productivity in the OR, a major revenue center in the organization. This productivity goal was woven in with the institutional grand scheme designed to make their delivery of healthcare "sustainable," and a part of the plan to address this need included accomplishing tasks via itineraries executed with a parallel approach. Confusing notion, right?

This plan for the delivery of perioperative care dictated that all the members of the team were to engage in this intricate ballet which meant that all the parts were just going to be "doing their own thing" at the same time—as if choreographed in a dance in which they would each perform their roles separately—and yet, magically, they would all arrive at the finale simultaneously.

No, I was told, there was no time to be at the patient's side during the anesthesia induction because I would be busy with other chores; it made sense, I heard, because this was how we would increase productivity.

We would each complete more cases and, as a collective, we would improve the financial health of the institution. More money in the bank account would mean that the mission of the institution would be secure and could continue to expand. Sustainability was the new buzzword.

It would all add up in the end, and I wasn't to worry about small things such as comforting frightened patients or hand-holding because all the accounting numbers supported the new approach. No worries! Focus groups had met, studies had been completed, and it had been determined that this would all guarantee the future of the institution. The financial health of the institution was, after all, the foundation absolutely required to provide the continued availability of high-quality healthcare, the very same care that we would all be delivering in this parallel adventure.

Going beyond that, even more work would soon be done to see if there were other ways to nip and tuck the process to make it leaner, so that it would be even more productive!

And I hardly dared to ask where was the patient in all this "innovation?"

The patient?

Ah, yes! Well, they were no longer going to be the center of the universe in that room; there was no need to have everyone looking at the patient. That didn't make sense, after all, since what mattered now was the numbers, and the patients just had to get swept along in making the numbers fit. In short, the productivity figures would become the new sun in our healthcare universe. When I left that interview, I acknowledged that a little part of me had died by accepting the position in this temple of the modern healthcare industry. What had always given me the reason for going to work in the morning, my patients, had moved far away from the center of my universe.

***

Time to digress and look at something which many folks may take for granted in their daily lives: trees.

Trees are simply marvelous things and greatly underestimated.

I have been blessed with the opportunity to live much of my life surrounded by them. I have always appreciated how trees not only add richness to the landscape, but also serve many purposes in maintaining the balance of the ecosystem. They exist in a beautiful symbiotic relationship with the environment around them, providing shelter, health, food, and stability in nature. To live and grow, trees need nourishment, water, and sunshine. Residing in Northern New England, I have come to appreciate the strength of what surrounds me while also conceding that even the largest among them may be damaged by injury or deprivation.

The most obvious and easily viewed portion of the trees are the leaves.

These fluttering green beacons provide evidence of the tree's good health; they also are the home for the laboratory which makes, with the assistance of sunshine, essential nutrients for the tree (remember that old term, photosynthesis). We depend on this process since it cleans our air and produces oxygen, required by living things to breathe, as a byproduct.

The branches and trunk are the conduits of water and nutrients for the leaves, and for any fruit and seeds that the tree produces. In turn, these seeds are the key to assuring sustainability of the forest, whereby healthy trees are constantly replacing themselves into the future. Just think about the number of acorns that arrive in any given year; each acorn is a potential oak tree.

Now, we need to focus on the root of the matter... see what I did there? Indeed, it was done purposefully!

While they pass largely unseen, we need to talk about what is paramount in maintaining the fortitude of the rest of the tree–the roots. Roots afford access to minerals, nourishment, and water. As go the roots, so goes the rest of the tree. Roots not only provide for the tree, but they also give back to the soil in which they are planted. Without the presence of roots growing deeply into the earth as well as closer to the surface, the soil around them would simply erode when exposed to the forces of nature.

Healthy roots are integral to maintaining the stability of the landscape, something that not everyone realizes.

Trees may live to be quite old and yet continue to remain vibrant and beautiful in both form and function. They may also be exposed to pestilence, lack of nourishment, injury, and toxins that cause them to dwarf, wither, and possibly die.

I live in a place where, for several months of the year, harsh winter weather necessitates the use of snow plows and application of salt to the highways to allow traffic to continue safely moving. While necessary, these actions potentially cause trauma and the run-off of toxic chemicals, which ultimately have a significant impact on the woodlands. High winds, ice storms, and blizzards take a toll on my forest friends, too. And of course, humans tread on the lives of trees, as well. The majority of us have seen the sad results when a vehicle has met a tree at high speed.

The landscape may look very different from year to year, yet the forest continues to survive because of those wonderful seeds, which were grown and diligently dispersed, seemingly in anticipation of the impending threats to their species' survival.

You may be wondering how this forestry lesson relates to healthcare?

Well, it's because in a rather round-about way, the structure of a tree has become the outline for this book. I toiled away at making a traditional outline, replete with numbers and letters. It seemed thoughtful, sure, but almost too structured. Then, I moved on to a big poster board with multiple rectangles and lots of differently colored sticky notes. That outline provided what looked like an impressive arts and crafts project. It seemed to take on a life of its own, without giving me the function that I required.

Anyway, one brisk morning, as I was sitting on the porch drinking coffee, the trees at the edge of the yard caught my eye. I saw that one of the very pretty birch trees near the road had obviously had a very tough winter; it was apparent that half of the branches would not be leafing out ever again, and that sadly, something was wrong with some of the roots. The end result was the easily observable deleterious impact at the top of the tree. *Hmm*, I thought, *this is similar to what my gut tells me is happening in healthcare today.*

If we go on with this analogy, we see that the roots that nourish and anchor the healthcare tree are varied. The deep, sustaining roots are made up of patients, healthcare workers, culture, organization, science & technology, and heritage. If any of these roots fail, there is an impact on the rest of the tree.

Moving up the anatomy, the tree trunk is the conduit allowing the flow of sustenance from the roots, to maintain health and equilibrium all the way to the branches, leaves, and seeds found at the top. This is the here and now of healthcare. The trunk of the healthcare tree is exposed to all manner of great and dreadful influences during the actual business of healthcare. In recent memory, stressors which quickly come to mind include, but are not limited to: advances in technology; political agendas; the ever-dwindling supply of healthcare workers; access to care; high cost;

the price of healthcare education; healthcare disparity/uninsured consumers; violence; and—of course—now, a pandemic. These all have besieged the healthcare tree.

Turning our eyes in the direction of the leaves and seeds at the top of the tree, it is clear that the continuous challenges have had an impact on present healthcare delivery and future sustainability. From where I sit, this tree needs some help soon in order to survive. The roots are struggling and the leaves at the top are dying.

Whether we call them patients, consumers, or clients, the name isn't important; it's the role that is paramount. This group must be the center of the healthcare universe. Without patients/consumers/clients, there would be no reason for healthcare to exist. It is exceptionally rare in the U.S. to find someone who has never had any experience of receiving medical care, and based on this, I feel that it is safe to assert that we all are impacted by the end result of the influences, which promote or diminish quality healthcare and its delivery.

That bears saying again, we are ALL impacted by what happens within the healthcare tree. I love that saying, "What happens in Vegas, stays in Vegas." It's so clever and ever so easily transferable to many situations in life. Yet this trite phrase—usually spoken with air quotes around it—grants permission to shut the door on situations and not look back.

Believe me when I tell you that this handy little sentiment, along with the accompanying attitude of disengagement when applied to healthcare culture and delivery, will not serve ANYONE well.

What happens in healthcare cannot be contained behind a closed door – the impact surrounds and affects each and every one of us.

While my intuition may be spot on, and despite the fact that I said I wouldn't get engrossed in statistics, I did look for supporting data to provide quantitative validity of this point. Many people simply won't believe something if they don't see an array of associated numbers, and the impact of allowing a continued decline in healthcare provision is important enough to go find those numbers.

So, I did.

My purpose is not to provide a scholarly dissertation on the current state of healthcare; many peer-reviewed professional journals have done the studies, collected the statistics, and offer the opportunity for a more complete review of the issues presented here. These issues are always evolving. I encourage you to do further research if you are inclined to dig deeper into any of the topics discussed. Knowledge is power.

Doctors

One deep root that I need to examine is the state of healthcare workers, specifically, physicians and nurses. I feel that in my time in nursing—plus as a life-long consumer of healthcare services—there has been a challenging shift in the environmental pressures impacting professions involved in the delivery of healthcare. I do not mean to neglect the other key components of the healthcare team. It takes each and every person in an organization or institution to keep the gears of the machinery turning. However, I will direct my attention to the doctors and nurses because those professions provide the vast majority of data for review. But remember, what affects one part of the tree roots often will impact the rest of the tree without any prejudice or forethought.

I would like to start at the beginning.

Let's think about the pile of cold cash required to pay for an education. It is a rare person who attains a medical school diploma without taking out educational loans. Not only does the price of tuition add up, but assorted fees and exams top off the bills in medical school. For many medical students, living expenses must also be covered by loans. After all, not everyone can live in a relative's basement while attending medical school.

According to the National Center for Education Statistics, the following amounts are averages for total educational (undergraduate and medical school) debt:

For the class of 1999-2000: $127,500
For the class of 2015-2016: $251,600

That's an increase of 97% — even after adjusting for inflation. Simply staggering.

Looking at just the loan debt for medical school for those graduating in 2019, we gain a clearer idea of the wildly enormous financial undertaking of a medical education for recent graduates:

Looking only at members of the class of 2019 who borrowed to get their medical degree, the American Association of Medical Colleges (AAMC) broke down how many borrowed how much for medical school:

Borrowed less than $150,000: 28.3%
Borrowed $150,000 to $299,999: 53.5%
Brrowed $300,000 or more: 18.1%

Not only is there the principal of the loan to repay, but also, there's the interest that accrues on it. After medical school graduation, there are still more years to work in gaining skills and experience in the "on-the-job" training in residency and fellowship programs. For many resident physicians, opting for repayment plans based on their income are the only feasible options to continue paying their loans while still having money for food, transportation, and housing during residency training.

What are physicians in training paid? The average annual income for a resident in 2019 was $61,200. This was a 3% increase over the previous two years. Residents in the U.S. are legally restricted to working no more than eighty hours a week as mandated by the rules of the Accreditation Council for Graduate Medical Education. Based on an eighty-hour work week, that average salary boils down to a whopping $14.70/hour before taxes and benefits are taken out.

Opportunity cost is one of those ideas that I had to learn about in my Economics 101 class. Simply defined, it is the cost of what is lost in order to pursue an opportunity.

If we think about it in terms of physicians, we can fabricate an interesting example of what the opportunity cost of pursuing medical education and training looks like.

Let's say that your daughter is finishing her junior year in her undergraduate program, and she is on her way to medical school after graduation. Her plan is to pursue a residency, which will take five years and a two-year fellowship after residency.

Her twin sister plans to start working in an accounting firm directly after she graduates with her undergraduate degree.

What is the opportunity cost for the twin headed to a career in medicine? It will be eleven years of school and training before she starts to make a "regular" income. What would she have been making if she had joined her sister at the accounting firm? Let's say that her numbers-savvy accountant sister will make an average salary of $75,000 a year working for the four years that her twin was in medical school and not earning any income. $75,000 X 4 = $300,000 is the very basic financial opportunity cost for our future doctor, based on what she gave up by attending medical school rather than heading off to the job market as her financially savvy sibling did.

Furthermore, the opportunity cost goes up significantly when including the years of reduced income during residency and fellowship training.

Adding the opportunity cost to the loan debt load gives a picture of the harsh financial reality facing new doctors today. It's a hard sell to convince someone to commit to this staggering financial burden combined with the brutal workload, wouldn't you say? Pursuing this goal takes real dedication and commitment.

But, after getting through all of this expensive education and exhausting training, life must surely be grand. One would think so, but the career of a practicing physician has many chances to go off the rails.

For instance, the 2017 Medscape Malpractice Report, discussed the results of a survey of 4,000 physicians across multiple specialties. While different specialties had variable rates of malpractice litigation, the results showed that, overall, 55% of the respondents had been sued for malpractice.

Does that mean that they were all found responsible for malpractice? No. Did they all have to defend themselves against the lawsuit? Yes. That is a mountain of work and income for the lawyers dealing with medical malpractice, isn't it? And, of course, one of the gargantuan expenses associated with medical practice is malpractice liability insurance, something that is just one of the necessary requirements of doing business as a physician. The cost of the plan varies according to locality and specialty, but annual malpractice insurance premiums for some medical specialties can go as high as six figures.

Many would stereotype the lifestyle of a physician as being one of privilege and wealth. This may be true for some, but not all. The stresses of providing safe patient care, meeting productivity standards, and running the gauntlet thrown down by the healthcare industry all take their toll.

A couple of years ago, I arrived at work to find that the routine rituals that started the usual day in the operating room were in complete shambles. The entire anesthesia department had been taken away from the perioperative area for an emergency meeting. How were we supposed to get patients into the operating rooms on time if one of the major players, anesthesia, had gone missing in action?

As the members of that department began filtering back into the surgical area, it was apparent that they had just received some sort of devastating news. One of the nurse anesthetists literally dropped into my arms, sobbing. This was when the perioperative staff discovered that an anesthesiologist had died by suicide the evening before, and this particular anesthesia provider had been a favorite among all those who worked with her.

We had also been informed by the management team that we were to be in our rooms and ready to move patients in for surgery with no more than a fifteen-minute delay. Well, ten minutes of that delay had already been used by incidentally finding out about the death from the devastated anesthesia group. We all had literally five minutes to pull ourselves together and head into patient care. Five minutes. Red eyes, blank looks, teary faces were the norm.

Patients could see that something really bad had happened. One family wondered aloud if it was even safe to have surgery that day. For me, the icing on the cake materialized when I discovered that no one had informed the surgeons of the death of our colleague. They had not been told of the reason for the delay to the start of their day. Thus, at the end of the first case in my assigned room, the anesthesia and nursing staff were the recipients of a stern lecture from the attending surgeon who did not appreciate the late start on a day when he had a busy schedule. He hoped that we would keep our noses to the grindstone for the rest of the day since he didn't want his productivity numbers to be negatively impacted by our tardiness. Not long after our public dressing down, someone finally took the surgeon aside to break the news of the death.

After arriving home later that day, I headed out with the dogs for a walk. It had been a long, draining day. I felt empty and very disappointed in how this untimely death had been handled by a, theoretically, cutting-edge medical facility. A neighbor stepped out to greet me and observed that I looked horrible. After I offered up the bare minimum of the day's events, the neighbor looked at me aghast. The first words out of her mouth were, "Oh, how did she kill herself? Did they tell you?"

This was followed rapidly by, "Don't they screen you people for that?"

Wow. I now bypass speaking to this neighbor as much as possible. How is it that professions built on compassion and caring can receive so little in return?

Statistics on physician suicide are tricky. Overall, if a death occurs in a hospital or at home, information can be sorted in such a manner that the death may not go in the count for suicides. Even with the elusive data taken into consideration, the reality is that physicians die by suicide at a higher rate than the general population. After looking at some of the more recent information, I found that doctors die by suicide at a rate of between 28 and 40 per 100,000. How does this number stack up against the general population? Death by suicide occurs at a rate of 12.3 per 100,000 in the general population. By some estimates, physicians are dying by suicide by as much as four times the rate of the general population. Another way to look at this statistic: in the US, one physician dies by suicide every day of the year.

But, after this little overview of the medical profession, there are still lots of physicians to be had... certainly enough to go around and meet everyone's needs, right? Actually, that is not the case. In 2020, the Association of American Medical Colleges (AAMC) offered that there was a shortage of 29,000 to 42,900 physicians in our country.

The AAMC, a non-profit organization that oversees medical education, research, and patient care, has projected a shortfall of between 54,100 and 139,000 physicians in the U.S. by 2033. If health disparity were no longer an issue and the medically underserved were able to access adequate healthcare resources, this deficit of physicians would, quite possibly, increase significantly.

One of the political stumbling blocks to increasing the number of physicians is the 1997 cap on Medicare financial support for graduate medical education. There has been no legislation allowing an increase in funding for residency slots since 1997. As a result of this lack of attention to a looming shortage of physicians, very few slots have been added in over 20 years. A medical degree, without completing a residency program, is not enough to enter the world of healthcare. Without residency training spots in accredited programs, there is no opportunity to increase the number of physicians, regardless of the number of medical school graduates.

I would have to really ponder about choosing to pursue a career in medicine if I were a college student now. The stressful work environment, potential for legal liability, lack of support, financial burden, competition for postgraduate training spots, and a looming megalith of a shortage would not encourage me in the least.

If you want to look at other topics impacting physicians in the U.S., I have included a partial list to get you started on your research.

I would suggest that you take a look at the following:

- Substance abuse and healthcare providers
- Average age of physicians
- Productivity requirements for resident physicians in training
- Suicide rates of medical students
- Impact of shiftwork on physical health
- Influence of medical licensing requirements on physicians' access to mental health services
- What makes medical school tuition so costly

Nurses

And, now let's turn our attention to nurses. I have already pointed out the challenge of furthering education in nursing, but what about the cost of becoming a nurse? It is a rare student who graduates from college without any loan payments and nurses are no exception. I took a little look around and found these statistics on the debt burden for nurses.

The average nursing student debt depends on the type of program you attend:

- Associate Degree Nursing (ADN): $19,928 average debt
- Bachelor of Science in Nursing (BSN): $23,711 average debt
- Master of Science in Nursing (MSN): $47,321 average debt

Average monthly student loan payments are $196 for ADN RNs and $234 for BSN RNs. Nurses with an MSN face monthly bills of $544, on average. These average debt levels and payment amounts are based on an analysis of December 2019 federal student aid data from the U.S. Department of Education's College Scorecard.

Someone graduating with an ADN is, ostensibly, out in the workforce after only two years of school, thereby decreasing the opportunity cost associated with their education. That opportunity cost saved is, in my opinion, often unequal to the sacrifice of career mobility and advancement that many ADN graduates face due to the lack of a BSN. Here is another interesting statistic found in a 2019 survey published by Medscape: at age fifty-five, 20% of nurses are still making student loan repayments.

Every two years, licensed nurses in the U.S. complete a questionnaire that provides data for the National Nursing Workforce Study. This is the only national survey encompassing the entire nursing workforce, and as I write this, the results are being collected for 2020. Here are some interesting statistics to mull over from this source:

- The average age of RNs is *fifty-one*, consistent with the 2015 and 2013 study findings.
- Data indicates a growing number of male RNs; 9.1% in 2017, compared to 8.0% in 2015 and 6.6% in the 2013 study.
- 19.2% of RN respondents are minorities, which includes 'other' and 'two or more races.'
- 41.7% of RNs report a BSN as the degree that qualifies them for their first U.S. nursing license; this number was 39% in 2015, and 35.5% in 2013.
- Hospitals are the primary employment setting for 55.7% of RNs.
- The median pre-tax earnings for RNs have increased from *$60,000* in 2015 to *$63,000* in 2017.

I would like to draw your attention to the first and last items on the list. Please note that I have taken the liberty to italicize the numbers in both of those.

The average age of nurses is not going down; it is remaining steady. I would be willing to guess that not only are young people not joining the profession, but quite possibly, younger nurses are not being retained in nursing.

The last item on the list points to a fiscal challenge in nursing: wage compression.New graduates may feel flush with the salaries offered to them directly after being handed their diplomas. Over the years, however, it is not uncommon for the more seasoned nurses to realize that they are continuing to be paid wages quite close to those of recent graduates. In my decades of nursing, the average annual pay increase was normally in the 1-3% range.

There is an interesting phenomenon quietly occurring while most aren't paying attention. It is common knowledge that, in most areas of the U.S., the population is aging. Baby Boomers are slipping rapidly into what my father would have sweetly referred to as the "legion of old farts." It's safe to say that aging populations require more healthcare services. There is an inverse ratio of supply and demand occurring in society that should cause all of us a great deal of concern. Simply put, we see that as the older population increases, the quantity of available nurses is decreasing. We are sitting on the precipice of a magnificent shortage of nurses. It is estimated that the growth of an aging population combined with the exodus of seasoned nurses reaching retirement age will result in the need for 1.1 million new nurses by 2022 to avoid a shortage. My intuition tells me that this number will be more than impossible to attain and has been further complicated by the disruption caused by a pandemic.

Frontline nursing is not an easy job. The hours are long, and rotating shifts can be taxing for both nurses and their loved ones. The physical and emotional toll of the work can be enormous. Violence in the healthcare workplace adds to the stress and burnout in an environment, which, on many days, resembles a pressure cooker of responsibilities.

Because of their proximity and amount of time spent with patients, nurses are among the highest risk groups for becoming victims of violence. PTSD, depression, anxiety, and substance abuse are just some of the deleterious complications that may accompany working in a profession that cares for the very sick and injured.

The topic of depression and its impact on nursing deserves a bit of time and attention. There are few among us who have not had some experience, either personally or vicariously, with depression. Depression rears its ugly head and is often seen as a conglomeration of symptoms. Those suffering from depression may find that sleep habits are disturbed, feelings of overpowering sadness and exhaustion are the status quo, concentration is difficult, and energy levels are low. If left unacknowledged and untreated, depression may become the stepping stone leading to death by suicide. According to my perusal of the literature, it is estimated that nurses suffer from depression at twice the rate of the general population. Interestingly, I found that much of the information about the issue of depression affecting nurses segued frequently with another important topic: patient safety. When looking at the symptoms of depression, it is not difficult to extrapolate the potential impact on safe and efficient patient care. In 2020, the first national study was published by University of California San Diego School of Medicine and UC San Diego Health, Department of Nursing regarding suicide rates of nurses. Not surprisingly, the longitudinal study revealed that nurses (both male and female) were at a significantly higher risk of dying by suicide than the general public.

Some topics you might want to research further include:

- On-the-job injury rates for nurses
- At-Will nursing employment
- Legal liability for nurses
- Employment retention for nursing
- Travel nursing industry and the impact on the cost of healthcare
- Occupational causes of depression for nurses

I know that every generation has struggles. My mother used to tell me about her terror of taking care of polio patients in a hideous, but life-saving, contraption known as an iron lung. Unimaginable in this day and age of intensive care units and ventilators, right? Healthcare workers continue to face troubling times. Not a day goes by that we don't hear about unsafe conditions, violence, lack of resources, and short staffing to name just a few of the nightmares facing the folks in the healthcare trenches.

I feel that one of the most discouraging pieces of practicing nursing is an overwhelming weight of responsibility for delivering safe patient care with little or no voice in making positive changes. Would I do it all over again? Would any of the nurses whom you know do it all again?

The Healthcare Industry

Now it is time to turn our attention to one of the main roots in healthcare: the industry. From my vantage point, I would assert that this root winds itself in and around the patient, physician, and nurse roots. The healthcare industry controls purse strings, work environment, and employment security for many nurses and doctors. It also has an enormous influence on cost and accessibility of healthcare services for those it is meant to serve.

While I won't spend much time on it, the drug industry also has roots twisting in and around the healthcare tree. You may want to spend a bit of time perusing to see what you might learn about the following topics:

- What does the average American family spend on prescriptions annually?
- What is the annual profit of the drug industry?

- What is the average number of prescriptions written per patient annually in the U.S.?
- What is the average annual out-of-pocket cost paid by consumers for prescriptions?

Back to the business at hand: the healthcare industry. Whether you have availed yourself of healthcare resources in public, non-profit, or for-profit facilities, you may have noticed similarities existing across the board. Healthcare is big, big business. Huge, even.

The best source I found for gaining an overview of the state of hospitals is the American Hospital Association (AHA). This organization has been in existence for a little over 100 years, providing support and working to maintain political leverage through aggressive lobbying on behalf of its members. According to the AHA 2018 survey, there were 6146 hospitals in the U.S., with a total 924,107 staffed beds. This simply means that there may be more physical beds present, but no staff to provide care for any patients filling them. I liken it to the situation we have all experienced when arriving at a restaurant with many empty tables, but we still have to wait for a seat because there aren't enough waitstaff to provide service if more of the seats are filled. The AHA established that the total expenses in 2018 for all hospitals was a whopping $1,112,207,387,000, and the total number of 2018 admissions was 36,353,946. As I said, big business.

Many hospitals are nonprofit organizations. I think that it is safe to say that most consumers feel any nonprofit organization must have been established to help the needy, provide necessary services to the world, and generally do good. This sort of entity must surely put every precious coin in the cash box back into the system to continue with their beneficent work. Many nonprofit hospitals encourage charitable donations and actively participate in aggressive fundraising campaigns. Obviously, they need all of our support and pocket change to survive, right? But, really, where does some of this heap of cash go? Sharing some of the high points of what I learned in my reading may prove enlightening for you:

A big pile of cash goes to the executives with corner offices located on the mahogany hallway at the non-profit organizations. Take a look at how the compensation breaks down at the 82 largest nonprofit hospitals in the U.S. using recent IRS 990 informational returns and auditing:

- 13 organizations paid their top earner between $5 million and $21.6 million
- 61 organizations paid their top executive between $1 million and $5 million
- 8 organizations paid their top earners less than $1 million

In addition to the executive paychecks, it is important to remember that various perks are usually included in the compensation package for those working at the top of the hospital budget food chain. Severance, paid vacations, travel, housing, professional meeting fees, gym memberships, and transportation allowances are just a few of the extra options. The compensation of upper-level management in these hospitals is only a scratch on the surface of where the cash is funneled in non-profit hospitals. Political lobbying to promote the interests of hospitals may also dip into the purse.

Patients

Time, at last, to turn our attention to what I believe to be the most important root of all: those we serve.

Without patients, healthcare would have no reason to exist. I believe it is safe to say that patients make up the most critical root of the healthcare tree. So, how do they fare in the healthcare industry arena?

Healthcare expenses take a large bite out of the family budget. It has been estimated that the average American family spends in the neighborhood of $20,000 annually for health insurance premiums, deductibles, and out-of-pocket medical expenses. There is little to be done by the consumers of healthcare to either negotiate the price of care or budget for unexpected medical emergencies. Give it a try to figure out how much your bill will be at your local hospital for a routine procedure such as a total hip replacement. Where do you start? Who do you call? What answers did you receive? I'm afraid that you may be disappointed with the lack of transparency.

For many people, health insurance is a benefit attached to employment. Many find that even though they have health insurance, they also have enormous deductibles. These deductibles must be met before coverage kicks in to cover costs. There are yet other employment options that don't come with the opportunity to participate in an employer's health insurance plan. Depending on income and assets, some patients may be able to gain access to Medicaid assistance in order to receive healthcare coverage. However, not everyone who needs health insurance meets the qualifications for public assistance; the net has large, gaping holes through which individuals and families frequently slip.

In 2018, the U.S. Census Bureau reported that 27.5 million Americans had no health insurance. I think it will be horrifying to see how many more have become uninsured in 2020-21 due to political maneuverings, the COVID-19 pandemic, and economic challenges.

Access to affordable healthcare is a challenge for many. Illness and injury may have catastrophic financial consequences for many American families. The goal of practicing preventative healthcare and patient education is unattainable for many providers due to heavy workloads and productivity requirements. Patients make up a main root for the healthcare tree and this root is, in fact, struggling to access and pay for adequate healthcare.

Conclusion

Let's stray back to my tree analogy to wrap up this discussion. I am not an arborist, but from where I sit, the healthcare tree is definitely not looking very robust. Frontline providers and patients, two of the very important roots feeding the tree, are faced with multiple challenges; some of them almost seem insurmountable.

In my opinion, the "industry" has taken a divergent path from the ethical and moral principles on which its foundation was built. It would almost appear that some roots are choking the life out of the others. Leaves are withering and fewer seeds seem to fall for future growth.

Therefore, unless there's some radical feeding and the administration of essential care very soon, I think that the future outlook and prognosis for the healthcare tree does not look promising.

Bullet Journal #3

Give yourself time to think about the changes that you have seen during the time you have been working in healthcare. Without assigning judgment, please list four of these changes:

-
-
-
-

What are four initiatives that you would support to maintain the sustainability of compassionate, accessible healthcare? Let your imagination run wild with this.

-
-
-
-

Chapter 5:

*Hannah**

Hannah: Hebrew for "Grace of God"

Hannah works the overnight shift, or, as you may have heard it called, the graveyard shift. We spoke on her day off. I remember how it felt trying to stay up, with little or no rest, on the first day off after working a run of night shifts. As I recall, it felt very similar to that college experience that so many of us have nursed ourselves through—the morning after a Saturday night party.

Or it's like the sense of struggle felt while reconnoitering the required daytime schedule of events after being up all night with a sick child. If there is any hope for getting exposure to the light of day and joining in normal activities with that portion of the civilized world that enjoys working while the sun is up, the night-shift worker must dance a fine line between perpetual jet lag and becoming a total creature of the darkness.

As we spoke about her thoughts and ideas of life as a nurse, Hannah struck me as someone who has learned to finesse this balance. She comes across as determined, stalwart, and solid in her beliefs and values. She is also open to introspection with a healthy dose of honesty.

As with many others who become nurses, Hannah did not have a direct trajectory into the profession. She always just knew that she wanted to help and care for people.

Her original goal was to pursue education to become a physician or physician's assistant. In the interim, she spent three years working as an emergency medical technician (EMT) and certified nursing assistant (CNA). Through these experiences, she found that her path was leading her straight into nursing. Hannah's next step involved applying to and completing an accelerated nursing program.

Of the people I interviewed, Hannah is one of the youngest survivors of workplace violence. She has been a nurse for less than ten years and has learned a great deal about not only caring for patients, but also what it feels like to be the new kid on the block.

After graduating from nursing school, Hannah accepted a position working the night shift on a neurology/neurosurgery unit that was part of a receiving center for patients with traumatic brain injuries (TBI). To take this job, Hannah had to move away from her family, friends, and her church community, but it seemed a small price to pay to take advantage of the benefits that this opportunity was sure to offer her. She was excited to spread her wings and learn about caring for this challenging group of patients.

It was at this job, far away from her well-loved support systems, that Hannah was served her first bitter taste of violence. Aggressors can be found in many different areas in healthcare. Fresh-faced and in her first nursing position, Hannah "double dipped" from the tub of workplace aggression.

Hannah's introduction to the physical violence existing in healthcare happened abruptly one night while she was caring for a patient with a TBI. As Hannah was quick to point out, these patients may become exceptionally volatile at a moment's notice. This particular patient suddenly became very angry, and the hostility was being directed toward Hannah. Without warning, the patient sucker-punched Hannah squarely in the throat. Hannah remembers the panic caused by suddenly not being able to breathe without difficulty. She also recalled a sense of bewilderment; she quite simply could not grasp that this had even happened to her. She was there to care for and help this patient to heal; not to be beaten.

This bright young nurse learned a great deal from her maiden voyage in healthcare workplace violence. Management was not at all interested in what had happened to Hannah or the effects that the violence had on her. The only question asked was, "What could you have done differently to prevent the attack?" The shift to co-opt the victim into being responsible for the assault had started that day. Hannah offered that this response by management has helped to normalize the notion that experiencing violence is just a part of the job. Somehow, she was the one being held responsible for the violence having occurred, and she would simply have to learn to live with it. In retrospect, it almost had the flavor of industrial strength gaslighting – Hannah was the problem, not the institution.

During our conversation, Hannah mentioned seven different episodes of physical assault during her time in nursing. Three of these attacks left her with permanent injuries, which continue to cause discomfort.

This chronicle of workplace violence does have a few positive chapters. The last physical assault that Hannah experienced at the hands of a patient had a different ending from the others – finally, a bit of sweetness to balance out the load of bitterness. She referred to it as a "novel experience." In comparison to the post-assault response of management in the past, this time, she felt "completely taken care of."

What did that look like?

Once again, she had been injured by the violent behavior of a patient. However, this time, there was a surprising breath of fresh air in the response by her manager. Instead of assigning blame and shame as others had done in the past, Hannah shared that this manager was more encouraging and supportive of her. Hannah had immediate access to important resources and was given time to heal properly. Accommodation was made so that she could return to work doing what is known as light duty rather than having to settle in immediately to the heavy lifting of her regular position.

This turnaround made Hannah realize that her previous work atmosphere involved just a repetitive pattern of hostility where staff members were physically and emotionally at risk for violence, and given no assistance when it occurred. There is no doubt this kind of thing eats away at the joy gained from caring for patients, especially true when staff members receive little or no support from management after an assault—soul sucking, really.

I remember the terror of being a new nurse. I, too, was away from my friends and family, and it was one of the most challenging and stressful times of my life. Suddenly, I was thrown into situations for which nursing school had not at all prepared me, and I was trying to make my way in a hospital that was very different from where I went to school.

It was a sad, lonely time and felt as though I had been jettisoned into an unfamiliar and very hostile world. Hannah had experienced all of this and a little extra. She quickly learned what it felt like to be a victim of lateral violence. My heart broke a little for Hannah as she recounted some of her experiences as a new graduate nurse. I cringed while listening to Hannah's stories about her early days working the night shift in the hospital. As much as it pains me to write this, some nurses justifiably deserve the reputation of "eating their young."

"What am I doing wrong?"
~ *Hannah, RN, new graduate*

Have you ever been in a situation where no matter how hard you tried to be perfect at what you were doing, you still weren't good enough? And, the harder you worked to do exactly what other people wanted you to do, the more mistakes you seemed to make? Eventually, did it almost feel as though the prophecies of your critics become your reality through no fault of your own, and through no lack of trying to win the critics over in order to succeed?

Did it feel as if the aggressors in this scenario held all the power in every situation?

Hannah's first nursing position quickly developed into a recurring nightmare of this cascade of violence. Add in that she was living far from those who loved her and was working the night shift, thus isolated from any support to be found in the light of day.

There are so many ways to segregate staff. Old and young, opposite shifts, and varying educational and experience levels are just a few of the doors that open, allowing lateral violence in to sow its ugliness. Hannah discovered that while she worked diligently to find her groove on the night shift, each morning she was faced with the hostility of some of the day shift staff members.

She worked hard to increase her abilities in nursing and adapt to her role. I asked if she'd had a mentor who took her under their wing. Sadly, the answer to this question was no. She said staffing was so short on the night shift that it was truly 'every person for themselves.' The workload was heavy, and it was more a matter of just getting through the shift than helping Hannah to grow and embed herself into the work culture. Hannah was terrified to give the hand-off report in the morning since two of the day shift nurses were ready and waiting to criticize and humiliate her.

Her patient records were scoured for mistakes and then written up and given to management. Discipline, rather than education, became the norm. Trying to meet unknown expectations is stressful, rather like attempting to play an intricate game without knowing the rules. She regularly found herself the recipient of verbal abuse by other staff members – often in front of staff, visitors, patients, and families. Allies? None.

I would offer that Hannah is a strong and determined nurse; how else would she be able to continue showing up to care for patients in this environment? In spite of that core determination, Hannah began to suffer from an overwhelming sense of anxiety related to her workplace and the treatment she received at the hands of her co-workers.

What happened next conflicted Hannah deeply. She admitted that she "turned into a bully" too, and that she hated this about herself. Looking back on this time in her life, Hannah was insistent that it is important to make sure we "underscore the serious consequences of lateral violence, which are becoming a bully yourself, leaving the profession entirely, and/or [suffering from] psychological effects such as anxiety, depression, or PTSD."

She clearly stated that it is monumental to understand these outcomes are the direct result of lateral violence. Hannah realized that her behavior was changing as the lateral violence against her continued; she had now become the wounded healer who had learned to feel some sense of power by bullying a nursing assistant on the night shift.

This story of the impact of lateral violence doesn't end here, though. Hannah was able to do something quite remarkable. After taking time to think about the lateral violence she had experienced, and by understanding the mark that it had left on her—plus her behavior that was perpetuating lateral violence toward a coworker—Hannah realized that her original indoctrination to the workplace had resulted in a hugely negative impact on her ability to work well with colleagues. She made a decision based on this realization: she mindfully and purposefully changed her aggressive behaviors. Finally, the cycle of lateral violence was about to end for Hannah.

I need to pause here and simply say that Hannah is my hero. I understand that her first job had to have been similar to enduring a little slice of hell. It is easy to be caught up in feeling badly about the victim becoming the perpetrator, but I would like to affirm that self-compassion and forgiving oneself is key to growing and changing. Hannah has since completed a nurse educator program. She has also written and delivered a presentation to prevent lateral violence in the workplace.

There is elegant beauty in how Hannah has changed her approach in the workplace. When working with new staff, she goes out of her way to learn about them, their families, and their culture. She finds that she is protective of the nursing assistants and endeavors to reduce their risk of being injured by violence. She also makes a regular point of communicating how grateful she is for their help in caring for patients.

What is driving Hannah to continue on this path? Partly, it is her deep and abiding faith that keeps her going. She also emphasized that, "nursing is so much more than just watching out for patients... we need to make sure that we aren't missing out on the humanity of the patients and of each other."

As we finished our conversation, Hannah expanded more fully on this idea of recognizing the sacred part that makes up each person's humanity. She pointed out that we all need to take a step back from making assumptions or judging other members of the healthcare team. While it's easy to make snap decisions about others, it is far more graceful if we just take time to utilize understanding and empathy. Strong words. But true.

*Name changed at interviewee's request for anonymity.

Chapter 6:

*Glenda**

I found Glenda by way of serendipity. Back in seventh grade, I learned from my science teacher that serendipity could simply be defined as luck + knowledge. Glenda's name serendipitously popped up attached to a blog she had written on healthcare workplace violence. Luckily for me, this appeared while I was searching for information about an entirely different topic. My good fortune continued when she immediately responded to a request for an interview about her experiences. I was humbled by the eloquence and depth of feeling Glenda expressed during our conversation, but I was also deeply saddened by the harsh realities which have left an indelible imprint on this nurse.

My first impression of Glenda during our video meeting was one of calm intelligence, a welcoming warm smile, and a get-down-to-business demeanor.

My initial thought was *this is a woman who steps in and knows what to do*. First impressions are often telling and I was not wrong with this one.

I'm always interested in what inspires someone to pursue a career in nursing. It is a competitive college major that doesn't provide an open acceptance; some are called, and few are chosen. Matriculation in a nursing major is grueling. Glenda, like many other nurses, committed to this rigorous course of study after time spent working in a related field. When asked what had been the driving force that pushed her to pursue a career in the field of nursing, she simply said, "Being able to help people."

Glenda spent six years straight out of high school working as a home health aide. Home health aides are some of the unsung heroes of healthcare, providing the in-home support and care that enables many people to remain in their own homes rather than being moved into the structured setting of an institution. The work is hard, the pay is poor, and there is little or no chance for advancement. Yet, home health aides provide a vital service that many of us will require in the future. Glenda is forward-thinking and likes to challenge herself to grow. Nursing seemed a natural step to an expanded role combined with better compensation and the potential to broaden her practice.

During the ten years since receiving a BSN, Glenda has worked in what many would consider challenging areas: outpatient clinics, corrections, acute rehab, and neuro intensive care. Neuro intensive care is a heavy hitter (no pun intended) in terms of nursing skills. An almost intuitive finesse is needed to provide care to patients in this environment, and subtle changes in condition may require immediate intervention to thwart a devastating outcome. Glenda pointed out that delivering this sort of nursing care could be mentally exhausting, and it takes very little effort to imagine that it would be. At this point, I saw a bit of fierceness added to the mix of calm competence.

Glenda has a true passion for healthcare promotion. She values being proactive rather than reactive, and, in her words, she enjoys, "taking time to educate patients." Many of the patients for whom she has cared have suffered life-changing events as the direct result of a lack of health promotion and disease prevention, combined with a sense of disempowerment over their own health.

Patients may experience a disconnect between hearing and comprehending the plan of care. Implementing a change in behaviors needed to stay healthy is often beyond challenging. Lack of support, resources and access to care makes health promotion elusive for many in our country. Thus, understanding the rationale for the change is truly the first step in making that change happen. It is difficult for patients under stress to actively partner in working to be healthy if they don't have all the information about what they might do to take better care of themselves. Glenda is committed to making the connections count by handing her patients the power to make choices about their health, through educating them.

Simply delivering a prescription for pills without offering to patients the necessary tools to understand the benefits and side effects of that medication goes against the grain for Glenda. Plus, she prides herself on informing the patients about the steps required to promote health through lifestyle changes. Knowledge is power, and sharing the knowledge to empower patients to improve their health is a sacred obligation. She is the sort of nurse I would like to have by my side and advocating for me if faced with a personal health crisis.

Now, you probably guessed that workplace violence has impacted Glenda's nursing practice; she finds herself far more guarded when delivering care. I asked what she has learned from her time providing direct patient care, and Glenda offered, "In nursing, you advocate for everybody but yourself. Nobody stands up for you… when something goes wrong, the nurse is usually the scapegoat."

Having an epiphany may be defined as an experience of a sudden and striking realization. Glenda certainly had an epiphany on the day that she was caring for a patient who grabbed her by the scrubs while yelling verbal threats at her. Fortunately, she was not physically injured. Her soul was scarred by the assault and its aftermath, however – permanently scarred.

After the assault occurred, Glenda approached her co-workers and manager still shaken by the violence. People with whom she had spent long shifts working stepped away. No one offered support for or validation of her safety concerns. Not one co-worker. Management's response involved questioning Glenda about what she could have done differently that could have prevented the assault. The victim of violence, Glenda, instantly became the scapegoat for allowing it to occur. Somehow, it was her fault that she had been attacked, and she should have been more careful, or should have done this or that action to prevent it from happening—ridiculous assertions.

Her request to change assignments was denied, so she was forced to continue caring for the patient who had assaulted her. I asked what would have been helpful in the moment. She responded, "I wish that there was some sort of a 'nurse advocate' who could have supported me when this was happening. I don't know, though… I wonder even if such a thing existed if it would really work or just be for show on the part of the employer."

Ahh, there is that old conundrum of "spirit of the law versus letter of the law," right?

Glenda is a smart, well-educated nurse who possesses the capability to process a situation quickly using critical thinking skills. When asked, she stated her epiphany succinctly:

"This is a business and I am disposable."

Simple. Ouch. Despite that, Glenda remained keen on being proactive in managing challenges. Her frustration is visible when she speaks about the lack of training and protocols in place for preventing or dealing with an episode of patient aggression. This makes me feel sad, indeed, that a nurse who is a strong patient advocate finds herself without anyone to do the same for her.

What was the end result? Glenda stated, simply, "My days at that job were numbered after that."

We spoke about Lynne Truxillo, the nurse whose death initially brought Glenda and me together. Glenda wondered aloud, "I think about Lynne's co-workers... did they have any time to grieve? Were they given the opportunity to go to her funeral? What scars do they carry since Lynne's death?" These were all queries driven by a profound sense of empathy and compassion. It would be interesting to know the answers to those questions, wouldn't it?

We also discussed our concerns for frontline colleagues caring for patients during the COVID-19 pandemic. Lack of personal protective equipment (PPE), fear of catching a deadly disease, and watching patients die horribly and alone is taking an immeasurable toll on the mental health of healthcare workers. Glenda and I both wondered what would be done to help with the sequelae of this pandemic horror show. Would space be made and support available to help the healthcare workers to heal? Or to help them be safer when the next public health disaster arrives on our doorstep?

Glenda felt that unless we all speak up and demand better, she did not foresee any changes happening. She pointed out that often, the response of the industry is to push through and ignore the unpleasant issues because, "The show must go on." The bottom line is so very important, you see! More than healers' lives and souls?

At the end of our interview, I asked Glenda what her goals were for the future. I was truly eager to know, unsure that in her position, I could have carried on. My heart sank at her answer.

She was quick to respond that she did not see herself continuing in nursing. She saw that nursing did not provide the flexibility, culture, or climate that would give the foundation for the professional growth she craves. She will move on.

How many nurses like Glenda are we willing to lose in healthcare? And, to what end will this loss impact us all?

*Name changed at interviewee's request for anonymity.

Chapter 7:

Healthcare Workplace Violence

"Well, that's what you signed up for..."

Is it really what we signed up for when we chose a healing vocation? I certainly did not agree to be verbally or physically abused. Nor, do I recall a time when, as a student, workplace violence was discussed. In reality, healthcare workplace violence has become an epidemic that is not only ubiquitous, but also consistently tolerated within the hallowed hallways of healing. It is a pervasive, malignant, dirty little secret.

Healthcare is a violent environment. I offer no apology for the fact that I have said this before—nor for the fact that I shall probably say it again before the end of this book. I urge you to consider it carefully as a statement, and not just gloss over it.

To the uninitiated, it serves as quite a shock to learn that working in healthcare may offer a veritable smorgasbord of violent experiences on a daily basis. To many of the all-too-well-initiated, healthcare workplace violence is the stock and trade of working in a "healing" environment.

Ugh! How do I even begin to address this topic? Acts of violence provide a rich and varied experience. They are often glorified, abhorred, and accepted as the norm all in the space of a few moments. Everyone loves a "good" murder drama, don't they? Many love to read about the real-life exploits of an axe-wielding stalker, or a shooter gone crazy in a mall. Yes, sadly, it's true; many people enjoy watching and reading about all manner of violent incidents, even seeking them out.

Some would assert that violence exists as a natural part of our human condition. Therefore, we need to simply buck up, accept the consequences of it, and move on. My perspective about violence has been markedly influenced by being, quite literally, hit in the head by it. I remember the bitter, metallic taste in my dry mouth when I think about the abject terror that I felt as I became just another victim of workplace violence. I recognize that the fallout from it has significantly shifted my sense of safety and security in the world. As with many traumatic experiences, life *is changed* by violence.

It is best to start at the very beginning and step into a picture of what violence looks and feels like. TV shows and movies have offered us all a rich assortment of physical and verbal violence to enjoy vicariously from the safety of our living rooms; we can sit with our popcorn or ice-cream in our comfy chair, watching an assortment of violent acts—either filmed in real life, or dramatized.

We have the opportunity to watch a steady stream of people getting shot, beaten up, knifed, strangled, raped, beheaded, screamed at, threatened, and stalked via a whole variety of media platforms. The cast and characters may or may not survive, but at the end of the show, all the loose ends are tied up in a spine-tingling conclusion meant to satisfy both viewers and advertisers alike. Ah, if only real life could be so simple. The impact of the residual after effects of violence on the survivors are not nearly as tidy as the entertainment industry would have us believe.

Indeed, at the end of the documentary series about cops and the emergency services, in which a plethora of violent events and their aftermaths are often shown, we usually see (at best) a one-liner detailing what became of the patient or victim.

For example, *Jason, after being caught in an episode of gang violence, went on to recover from the knife attack he had suffered…*

He recovered? Did he really?

What does 'recover' really mean in this instance?

It probably means his bodily wounds healed—but what about his psyche? Can we call Jason healed when he is now too scared to go out of his own front door to go buy a carton of milk? Or when he cannot sleep due to nightmares?

Alas, the media glosses over violence all too easily, and we sit by and watch it all as entertainment. Or, read a well-written bestseller that is chock full of violence. Or, indulge with friends in a wildly violent video game. Remember, violence is ubiquitous.

To make the discussion of healthcare workplace violence more organized, I will attempt to sift through definitions, statistics, and impacts.

My father had a trite expression to describe statistical analysis: "Figures can lie and liars can figure." Remember Dad's quote as we delve into some of the issues around reporting and data collection.

In the arena of healthcare workplace violence statistics, there is an enormous potential for misrepresentation of the actual numbers of incidents occurring. These numbers are skewed by either a lack of reporting or the criteria established for an event to be reportable. The U.S. Bureau of Labor Statistics (BLS), Occupational Safety and Health Administration (OSHA), the Centers for Disease Control (CDC), The Joint Commission (formerly Joint Commission on the Accreditation of Healthcare Organizations—JCAHO), and some individual state-administered programs are all receptacles for healthcare workplace violence statistics.

There is not one single agency collecting *all* of the information about incidents of violence in healthcare. None. The criteria for documenting an episode of violence also may vary. Based on what I gleaned from the websites of the entities listed above, there are a few key issues regarding the collection of data that we need to acknowledge. Criteria for reporting may vary, too.

For instance, OSHA statistics are built around analyzing numbers of violent episodes resulting in time lost from work, yet OSHA only covers a fraction of all workplaces in the U.S. Sadly, productivity demands coupled with time constraints may cause staff to be reluctant to report occurrences. Workers may also hesitate to document episodes for fear of retribution from the employers or other staff. Victims of violence may not see any benefit in making a report if their experience has been one of lack of concern on the part of their employer. Why take time to report something if nothing is going to change—or, indeed, if you're only going to be held responsible for something over which you had no control?

I humbly request that you keep this background in mind as you read on through this chapter.

What is workplace violence? As defined by the U.S. Department of Labor, 'a workplace violence incident is a verbal, written, or physically aggressive threat or attack intended to intimidate, cause injury, or death to others in a place of employment.'

Please hold tightly to this all-encompassing description. I believe that it will aid you with the expansion of your view of what violent behavior really is in the healthcare workplace.

The National Institute for Occupational Safety and Health (NIOSH) lists three groups of risk factors that lead to violence in healthcare: (1) clinical (e.g., individual pain, fear, anger, altered mental status, history of violence, and the influence of drugs and alcohol); (2) environmental (e.g., layout, design, and amenities of the workspace); and (3) organizational (e.g., understaffing and long work shifts, inadequate security procedures and protocols, discouragement to report and difficulty in reporting violent incidents, acceptance by management and staff that violence is part of the job, and lack of staff training and preparedness).

NIOSH has broken workplace violence into four distinct categories:

- Type I: "Criminal intent" acts by persons having no relationship to the business or its employees
- Type II: Acts involving a customer, client, or patient with a relationship to the business, who is violent while receiving services
- Type III: Acts involving a worker-on-worker relationship (lateral violence) in which an employee attacks or threatens another employee
- Type IV: Personal relationship acts between a perpetrator and the intended target in which the violent act or threat occurs at the victim's workplace

Type II and Type III are my focus for this chapter.

I freely confess that healthcare workplace violence is a difficult topic to address. I have used the word "ubiquitous" to describe the prevalence of it earlier in this chapter. Ubiquitous means: present, appearing, or found everywhere. For those who have felt its cruelty, this may be a touch challenging to read. Personally, I have also found this chapter has been grueling to write. I confess that this is my third attempt at addressing it.

My fingers are crossed that the third time will be a charm. I have danced around the topic and worked to turn my thoughts into a narrative which described looking at violence in healthcare from a vantage point located somewhere on the very outer periphery. In the next round, however, I found that I was actually just writing a research paper full of facts and statistics—safely disengaged from any personal attachment to the issue. Neither of these approaches felt remotely true to the goal of this book... authentically sharing my experiences and what has been learned from them. This is not a scholarly academic work; these are merely my perceptions. I only ask that you keep an open mind while reading.

Please give yourself time and space to pass safely through the information about this topic. Some of the discussion will be uncomfortable, and you may have the stark realization that you are not only a victim, but that you also have been a perpetrator of healthcare violence in your workplace.

Understanding the results of perpetuating violence is a harsh realization. As that trite saying goes, "hurt people hurt people." I feel that those perpetrators of violence working in healthcare also deserve a healing space. To support you in this chapter, on this occasion, I am incorporating the bullet journal into the body of the writing rather than settling it at the end. Please, make use of it as it best serves you. My end goal is to give you space to grow and heal, not to judge or punish.

How do we manage this toxic entity in our workplace culture?

How do we continue providing care to needy, vulnerable populations when we are struggling with the experience of workplace violence?

I have found that people often rely on using words and platitudes to make sense of unusual situations, and this notion holds true for the conundrum of violence in healthcare. It is so hard to believe that such awful behaviors are readily integrated into what we would like to think of as a gentle, kind, and safe environment. Placating and minimizing phrases may be spit out without much thought or consideration for the impact on those affected by violence. For many, negating the emotional and physical injuries makes uncomfortable stories easier to file away in a locked closet. Assigning responsibility to the victim for being on the receiving end of violent behavior is also a nicely simple and convenient way to finish the discussion about an unpleasant incident.

After all, shouldn't a competent professional know how to manage any situation within the hallowed halls of healthcare? Turning an unpleasant narrative into a sassy little joke or critique often serves to make the nastiness more palatable. There, we made a joke about it and we all had a good laugh… and now it's all been laughed away and we can get on with the job!

It's really no big deal if we can laugh about it, right? Big, bold, brassy, nonchalant behavior after experiencing violence is akin to "whistling in the graveyard." Nothing can hurt me because I am a true badass… Just watch how tough I am.

As I was formulating the last paragraph, the following sentences surfaced in my memory. All of these words served to perpetrate, minimize, assign blame for, or justify acts of violence. These are some of the phrases that have been spoken in my presence at some point in my career:

"What did you expect? After all, those people are crazy."

"You fucking cunt…"

"Maybe if you just stood your ground, he would have backed down."

"What could you have done differently to have prevented this."

"You'll have to take care of him (assailant) if he is re-admitted to our unit; that's just what we do."

"Guns and knives? People only bring those to the hospital once in a great while."

"So, what did you do to piss him off and make him hit you?"

"Snitches get stitches…"

"Bitch…"

"Maybe if you had been a little quicker on your feet, you wouldn't have gotten hurt."

"Nurses love to eat their young."

"That was the way that I was trained and it served me well, right?"

"Nurses are their own worst enemies when it comes to workplace violence; they figure that it is just part of the job. They don't report it; that's why nothing ever changes to prevent it."

"Medical students, what a waste of space. They are so stupid…"

"You have to earn your stripes."

"Well, that's the way that we have always done it."

"I can't stand working with her; she's useless."

"Well, that's what you signed up for."

"Come sit next to me, I want to tell you what I heard about so-and-so today..."

If you have experienced violence in the healthcare setting, it's possible that you were made to believe it was a personal issue. I certainly felt this way. As I've gained some distance from my own experience, I have had the opportunity to gain a clearer comprehension of staggering vastness and multiple layers of workplace violence. I now view it as a systemic issue requiring a much greater understanding to allow change to occur in the healthcare workplace culture. A serious commitment is mandatory if we are to create and implement solutions to combat the damage it causes. I would assert that this commitment is imperative to ensure the continued sustainability of the caring professions.

Violence is, in fact, endemic to the healthcare workplace. It impacts many—if not all—areas of healthcare education and delivery. Shaming and blaming the victims has become a common response to healthcare workplace violence, and in some work cultures, it is seemingly the norm for post-episode debriefings to assign some sort of responsibility to the victim of the violence.

Anecdotally, I have heard from staff that after being educated about de-escalation techniques, they felt that the management of their facilities held them responsible to always be able to successfully manage violent episodes. If these skills weren't enough to calm the violent situation, the blame was assigned to staff incompetence. From my perspective, this is a very dangerous pathway for survivors, consumers, and the industry to choose to follow.

How can healing happen in any kind of a negative, violent culture? How do we make sense of our core belief of "do no harm" in an environment where we are physically, emotionally, and verbally abused, and in which we tend to see it accepted?

How do we mindfully shift our practices to increase the awareness of the violent behaviors covertly accepted as being a part of the workplace? Is it possible to adjust the culture of the healthcare industry to align with ethical mandates that support professional behavioral boundaries and expectations?

The harsh reality of some of the relevant statistics may be a bitter dose of truth.

Victims of violence do not exist in isolation; perpetrators are the necessary factors in the equation. Thinking about being a participant in causing harm or injury to a colleague opens up a wasps' nest of feelings, ideas, and attitudes. Allowing yourself space to sit in this snake pit of increasing self-awareness may not be easy or comfortable, and often, change is challenging. Acknowledging culpability and accepting responsibility for actions, even if that action is silence in the face of another's suffering, can be painful.

I encourage you to be honest and compassionate with yourself as you travel this path. As my mother would have pragmatically explained in this situation, "The truth isn't always nice, but it is still the truth."

Vertical Violence

One of my first memories of healthcare workplace violence occurred during a clinical rotation early in my nursing education. The nursing students in my program were all easily identified by our light gray/green, high-collared, action-pleated, three-quarter-sleeved uniforms; a design that was beyond grotesque to look at and extremely uncomfortable to wear.

In the early days of our first clinical experiences, the small group of students assigned to a patient care unit made sure to stick closely together. It would be accurate to say that we felt like tiny ducklings swimming around in a scary, dangerous pond teeming with hungry snapping turtles.

After each shift spent applying theory to practice by providing nursing care for patients, our instructor would lead us in a post-clinical discussion about what we had learned from the experience or what we felt we had done well. Or, in fact, the discussion might have been about what we had really struggled to manage and should most certainly brush up on before the next assigned clinical.

On this particular day, while waiting for our instructor, we were all initiated into one of the brutalities of working in a hospital—vertical violence. An impressive flock of white-coated demigods strode by our tiny gaggle. These were the power brokers of patient care: attending physicians, residents, and medical students. As they passed, we heard one of the residents order the medical student to stop by the nurses' station, find a patient chart, and write an order in it for the resident to sign. The medical student, driven to accomplish his goal and meet the expectation of his teachers, found the chart, plopped down in the nearest chair, and began to write with intent focus.

He had been charged with an important task and was, quite obviously, single-minded in his goal of accomplishing it. We all jumped as the ward clerk came around the corner and barked loudly, "Hey! What do you think you're doing? Get out of my chair!"

The medical student jumped up and backed away briskly. Horrified that he had been yelled at in front of an audience, he quickly apologized for his transgression. As the ward clerk pushed past him, she snapped, "I know that I'm pretty low on the food chain around here, but you are definitely a lot lower than me! Stay out of my space." Almost forty years later, I can still see the nasty sneer on her face. Just a rite of passage, right?

When uncivil behavior takes place between players on different levels in the hierarchy, it is known as vertical violence. These acts of violence may flow up or down the hierarchical structure. Nurses have been brutalized by the behaviors of physicians. Charge nurses have found themselves on the receiving end of abuse and bullying from staff. Conversely, managers have multiple avenues for denigrating those who work under them. For example, think about the annual evaluation process in most institutions. It is a time, for some, to look back at past accomplishments and future goals. Support and growth are the foundation for this experience. For others, the process is one of undermining, belittling remarks, and offensive attitudes directed toward them by their supervisors. These evaluations are interconnected with raises, promotions, transfers, and the opportunity for continued employment. This one event can be horrifically life-changing if the manager doing the evaluation happens to be a bully and is allowed to abuse their power unchecked by those above them.

Healthcare is a stressful work environment. There is so much pressure to not make errors and to be productive at all costs. Think about the learners still gaining experience in their chosen fields. My mind immediately turns to the interns and residents who work long hours for poor pay. Many of them are in situations where the attending physicians, who have been charged to instruct and guide, actually become the culturally accepted perpetrators of vertical violence.

These senior physicians hold tremendous power and influence not only over a resident's daily life, but also over his or her future career. While working a grueling schedule, this group of physicians-in-training are also the work horses who must maintain their supervisors' productivity goals. Brutal online evaluations, nasty comments in front of patients and families, or derogatory critiques with other staff can wear the learners down. It can easily become a pressure cooker seasoned with vertical violence for both interns and residents.

I have watched all of this happen in the goldfish bowl of the operating room. One surgeon with whom I regularly worked was so brutal in his treatment of both the residents and medical students on his service, that I would leave after a day of scrubbing cases with his team feeling as though my head would fly off my shoulders because it ached so horribly. Finally, not being able to face yet another twelve long hours of the behavior, I asked if I could chat with the surgeon at the end of my shift.

His response to my concerns about the impact of the tension and stress on the team was interesting. He felt that he was being kind in comparison to how he had been treated while in his own residency. He was confident that his behavior was a key factor in getting the house staff to do their jobs well. Being tough on them was just a part of the training that he lovingly offered to make them good doctors. Anyway, it couldn't be that bad; after all, nobody had gone up on the roof and thrown themselves off of it yet, he offered with a laugh. And, if someone did eventually throw themselves off the roof, I wondered who he thought that it would reflect on – him or them?

Bullet Journal #4

Describe some of the behaviors that you have seen displayed by staff toward students that make you feel uncomfortable.

-
-
-

How do you think the students felt during those interactions? Write three adjectives to describe what you think those feelings may have been.

-
-
-

What are some words to describe how you interact with students in your workplace.

-
-
-

How do you think another person might describe how they view your interactions with students in the workplace?

-

Lateral Violence

NIOSH Type III Workplace Violence

Perspective provides a bounty of insight into any situation. When I look at a situation from a more objective stance, it allows me to start peeling away the layers of what I am viewing. This objectivity also provides me with an opportunity to step outside of the notion that everything occurring in a situation is focused solely on me, myself, and I.

Peering into the eyes of the basilisk known as healthcare workplace violence allows me to understand that while some actions executed by this fearful monster are dramatically overt, others are so subtle that we easily slide into accepting them as simply a part of our heritage and culture. I believe that this is the case for what is known as lateral violence. The American Nurses' Association defines lateral violence as behaviors between colleagues, involving covert or overt acts of verbal or nonverbal aggression. Lateral violence, as it exists in and impacts the healthcare setting, deserves a closer look.

Many view nursing as a highly trusted and compassionate profession. It is humbling to think about the sacred trust placed in the hands of a nurse during a stressful health challenge. Healthcare workers in all areas are in the position of providing that supportive link which enables a glimmer of hope for healing to occur. Twenty-eight years later, I still remember the kindness of the nurse caring for me on labor and delivery while I was giving birth to my son. I also remember the housekeeper who compassionately listened to my frustrations and supplied a fresh box of tissues so that I could dry my tears. Over my years of practice, I have seen some of the very same sort of well-loved, competent staff engage in brutal acts of lateral violence directed purposefully toward their peers.

What I realize now is that much of this nastiness has become so routine that it often goes unnoticed and uncontested by peers and management; endorsed and accepted, it becomes who we are.

As I have said, lateral violence is, in some workplaces, simply the reality of everyday work life. It has been estimated that over 93% of nurses have witnessed some form of lateral violence in their workplaces.

Bluntly stated, lateral violence is pretty much a universal experience for nurses. The line between victims and perpetrators is both muddled and mobile. Often, the behaviors of the perpetrators are validated as being somehow justified not only by the person who is acting violently, but also by those witnessing the violence. After all, if people could just squeeze into the mold and were smarter, faster, or did things "the way that we always have done them," they could fit in better and not aggravate the old guard. Or, perhaps, if the old dogs in the pack would just go away, they wouldn't be the focus of humiliation or criticism. Who really cares about history anyway? Good computer skills and the ability to get through the technology challenges is the important priority, right? Just get the checklist done.

Again, it is the fault of the victim that this malignant behavior occurs. It feels important to not challenge the negative behaviors because those who don't support the aggressor run the risk of becoming future prey. We become accomplices in lateral violence by not challenging it, thereby helping to enable the continuation of it in the workplace culture.

So, what does lateral violence feel like?

Physically, it can seem that you can never take a deep breath or relax. You find yourself always on guard. Nausea, headaches, and other somatic complaints may surface. A feeling of constant exhaustion may creep in. Sleep quality may suffer. Anxiety may increase. Absenteeism may become problematic too, since it is easier to call out from work because of how awful you feel just anticipating what your day may bring. Loss of interest in activities that would usually make you happy when you are away from work—combined with either eating too much or too little—may be some warning flags for the onset of depression. Not wishing to get out of bed in the morning (or to start your new day, at whatever time it's supposed to begin) may also be a warning sign.

The sickening sense of isolation, uncertainty, and constant vigilance can be wearing. Add this toxic atmosphere to the equation of working to care safely for vulnerable clients/patients and it is easy to understand that lateral violence can be, literally, damaging to your health.

And what do the acts of lateral violence look like?

They are anything ranging from subtle to overt, all setting the stage to diminish and humiliate the victim. For example, picture yourself as a new employee walking into the break room for a cup of coffee before your shift starts. As you enter, all talking stops, and you realize that one of your co-workers is glaring at you. Nobody else at the table will make eye contact either, or you even hear a few stifled giggles. You wonder what you could possibly have done to elicit this response; and how to make it stop.

Or, perhaps this discussion makes you think back to being fresh out of school and starting your first job. Remember how scared and vulnerable you felt? Every part of your work environment seemed unfamiliar; even the smallest task required enormous effort. Now, picture yourself trying to do a hand-off to the next shift.

Listen to the people hearing your report criticizing and interrupting, while eye rolls and deep sighs punctuate the denigrating comments. And imagine that this happens every single day. This morning, just anticipating how it was going to feel to sit through a report made you feel like you might actually vomit, and you wonder how much longer you can do this.

Or maybe you're standing in the line to check out in the cafeteria, listening to the couple ahead of you gossiping about one of the other staff members on their unit. Hateful, vicious things are being said about the absent co-worker.

Why do people engage in lateral violence? What is the gain? I would offer that establishing a sense of power and control in a stressful environment may be the bait on the hook for some. Perhaps the perpetrators themselves have also experienced being bullied by co-workers in the past. Malignant behavior and attitudes may be demonstrated by management toward staff and that sets the tone for the workplace culture. It is even more difficult to address lateral violence if vertical violence is allowed to thrive in the environment. If people in leadership offer that lateral violence will not be tolerated, yet are viewed as bullies in their professional roles, their street credibility becomes null and void.

Bullet Journal #5

I have now heard about workplace incivility, lateral violence, and vertical violence. Working in healthcare is a tough job, and there have been times when interactions have caused me to wonder if they weren't a little over the top in terms of aggression.
Three situations that made me uncomfortable were:

-

-

-

List four words that describe your feelings around these situations – don't overthink or analyze… just write:

-

-

-

-

Physical and Verbal Violence

NIOSH Type II Workplace Violence

The issues of lateral and vertical violence in healthcare could take up multiple shelves filled with lofty tomes of learned literature. Anyone who has spent more than a minute in the healthcare workplace is bound to have an anecdote or example of some horror show where violence between the workers occurred. Now, it's time to turn our attention to the other group that brings violence to the healthcare workplace: consumers of healthcare services.

Our stage has been set with a well-embedded and accepted violent culture etched into the underpinnings of the healthcare industry. Now enter the main players in the continuing healthcare violence dilemma: the guests in our environment. These people are the very core of the reason that most frontline, direct-care providers continue to show up day after day; they provide us with the sacred opportunity to comfort, heal, and decrease suffering. Patients and their loved ones make up this pig pile of vulnerable, sick, injured, and struggling humanity that sits at the center of our universe. Yet, the statistics show that they are often the perpetrators of violent acts committed against healthcare workers in the workplace.

Remember that the data regarding the number of verbal and physical assaults is more than a little scattered. There are multiple databases utilizing varied criteria for reporting incidents. And then, not all assaults are documented. The Joint Commission has stated that only 20% of all healthcare workplace violence is reported. Some of the most telling information about rate and occurrence of violence comes not from reports of events, but from surveys conducted in the field with results analyzed in professional journals. For instance, The American Association of Critical Care Nurses (AACN) reported results of a study done in 2018, which found that 86% of those critical care nurses surveyed had experienced physical or verbal violence or sexual harassment in the prior year.

Methods for reporting incidents are not always accessible or easy to use. Managers may not validate or encourage the documentation of violence without a clear and viable commitment from upper-level administration. The atmosphere of concierge healthcare culture combined with institutional funding remaining dependent upon patient satisfaction surveys puts fiscal pressure on institutions to overlook whatever might damage its bottom line. The customer is always right. Taking a stand on aggressive patient behaviors is difficult when the money generated by those same people is needed to fill the industry coffers. Most frontline workers have little or no time away from patient care and productivity demands to document violence; it is just one more thing to do in an already busy environment. Much of what happens, unless there are significant injuries, is easily passed off as another day in the trenches of healthcare. If serious injuries do result from an assault by a patient, the window between patients' rights to confidentiality and privacy and reporting the event to law enforcement becomes foggy. The benefits of reporting an episode of violence in the workplace very often do not outweigh the damage that it can do to the victim. As I said previously, the first line of questioning is often directed toward establishing the cause of the event; it is simple to assign responsibility to the victim. What is the gain of documenting an episode of violence when nothing is done to rectify the situation—or, perhaps even more discouraging, when the reporting of it simply comes ricocheting back with blame assigned to the victim who reported it? This culture of silence does not allow the opportunity to collect data about healthcare workplace violence. If there is no data to support a problem, then the logical conclusion is that the problem must not exist, correct?

Remembering that not all violent incidents are reported; however, roughly 75% of 25,000 reported workplace assaults occurred in healthcare and social service settings according to the Occupational Safety and Health Administration (OSHA). Think about the fact previously stated that, according to The Joint Commission, only an estimated 20% of incidents are reported. When you consider adding the estimated 80% of violent incidents not documented, the numbers of healthcare workplace assaults have the potential to increase astronomically.

Bullet Journal #6

Have you ever witnessed a co-worker struggling with verbal or physical assault by a patient or visitor?

What words describe your feelings about this event?.

-
-
-

If you don't know the answers to the following questions, how might you find them?

How many documented cases of violence occurred at your workplace last year?

What is the mechanism for documenting an episode of either verbal or physical violence?

What is the standard procedure that occurs after such an incident is reported?

It feels as though we are attempting to build a jigsaw puzzle without access to the cover image or all of the pieces, doesn't it? How will this jigsaw ever get completed if the center piece and three corners are absent? What if the pieces don't seem to come together to fit any one image, and the whole picture cannot be seen anywhere? However, even then, the fragments may still tell us something.

So, let us think about some of the fractured numbers that have been collected. Even though they are fragmented, they still may help us to understand the magnitude of how this problem is evolving. And, while this data may not give us the truly complete shape or picture of the number of victims of healthcare workplace violence, it will provide some objective information regarding the magnitude of the issue, and the strength of feeling behind the issue, as well as of its acceleration and growth.

Let's take a look at verbal violence and its impact on the healthcare workplace.

Bullying was simply accepted as a rite of passage when I was a kid. The notion of emotional intelligence and compassion had not reached my elementary school back in the 1960's, and so bullying was not a topic addressed by parents or teachers. It was up to the victims to toughen up if they were to navigate through these experiences.

I remember a particularly rough day in fourth grade. I had been yelled at, threatened, and called names by a couple of classmates throughout the day, brutal, mean-spirited, ugly things that not only hurt my feelings, but also made me feel vulnerable and isolated. Kids can be horribly cruel. And the worst part? I had to go back the next day and live through it all over again.

I was completely trapped. The next morning, while waiting for the school bus, I told my father what had happened to me on the prior day. He simply shook his head and offered, "Well, that's just how people are. Remember, 'sticks and stones may break my bones, but words will never hurt me' and just ignore the bullies." Small comfort, indeed.

My father's somewhat feeble attempt to console me helped to lay the foundation for accepting verbal violence as a normal part of life. Now, I would argue, his attitude was far off the mark of the actual truth about the impact of verbal violence. Verbal abuse can and does hurt people. I believe that, when allowed to flourish, the effects of this behavior can fan the flames of aggression into physical violence.

How prevalent is the verbal abuse of healthcare workers? In a study undertaken by the American Nurses' Association published in 2014, 50% of the nurses surveyed had experienced verbal abuse in the previous twelve months. I would venture that this number has only increased in the years since that study was published.

In the beginning of my recovery from the workplace assault, I had an appointment with my primary care provider. She and I had a long-standing, cooperative relationship that spanned many years. During that particular visit, after we completed the list of issues needing to be addressed, we settled in and spoke about the assault that I had experienced. My physician offered that she worried daily that the verbal abuse that she often suffered during patient visits at that clinic would escalate to physical violence. And beyond that, if the verbal abuse progressed to physical assault, would she be able to get help or escape to safety? As a matter of fact, she volunteered, this concern had played into her decision to move out of the area to practice in a place with better security measures.

I ran across an interesting study, published in 2016, which demonstrated the rate of verbal abuse directed toward Emergency Medicine (EM) residents in the Emergency Department (ED). The results are telling. Sadly, 96.6% of the respondents in the survey reported being verbally abused by a patient. Visitors accompanying patients to the ED also spewed verbal abuse directed toward the physicians-in-training at the rate of 86.6%.

Sticks and stones can break your bones and words most certainly do have consequences. It is easy to visualize the additional stress that verbal abuse, sexual harassment, and threats of physical violence add to the already intense working environment of the emergency department. It takes little imagination to picture the end result being one of decreased job satisfaction and burnout. I would wager that the safety and quality of patient care have the potential to be diminished as a consequence of this epidemic of verbal abuse directed toward healthcare providers.

It is not difficult to understand that an environment laden with unmitigated verbal violence provides the fertile ground to cultivate the escalation of physical aggression directed toward healthcare workers.

And what about the impact of violence on patients?

The Emergency Department (ED) is the main receiving point for a rich assortment of patients. In most hospitals, the ED never closes. Unfortunately, the ED is also one of the most violent and dangerous areas in which to work; so exceptionally violent that aggression is often considered to simply be part of the job. The patients seeking care in most ED's sport a varied potpourri of diagnoses. Patients arrive urgently seeking help and care when they are sick, stressed, vulnerable, and with no other place to go for assistance. The American College of Emergency Physicians (ACEP) reported that 50% of Emergency Medicine (EM) physicians and 70% of ED nurses have been assaulted at work. In a follow up question, 80% of the ED physicians surveyed, not surprisingly, went on to assert that they feel that the violence negatively impacts the delivery of patient care.

I don't want to belabor the obvious point, but it deserves stating once again: healthcare violence impacts everyone.

A simple Internet search of "healthcare workplace violence statistics" will turn up a rich and varied sampling of information for reflection and discussion. Go ahead, take a look. There are plenty of sparks to ignite a fire focused on prevention and recovery, but very few flames have erupted thus far.

What is the impact of violence? The emotional, physical, and spiritual response in the moment varies, but common themes include shock, horror, disgust, feeling violated, isolation, confusion, shame, and pain. There is potential to get stuck in that sympathetic nervous system overdrive of fight-flight-freeze. Routine exposure to workplace violence, therefore, increases the likelihood of burnout, job dissatisfaction, staff turnover, and stress-related physical and mental illnesses. It also impinges on the ability to provide safe, high-quality patient care. For some victims of violence, it may precipitate the ending of their career in healthcare. Unfortunately, there is little discussed or written regarding support for the victims exposed to this malignancy.

Conclusion

I am still haunted by one of the last calls I received from the staff member assigned to me through the Assaulted Staff Assistance Program in my former workplace. I made the observation that, before the assault, I had worked fearlessly and tirelessly as a nurse. I was frustrated, angry, and discouraged that these attributes had been literally beaten out of me by both the patient and my workplace. The ASAP volunteer was quick to suggest that perhaps I should have been more afraid.

She mounted a last-ditch effort to convince me that I was remiss by not having an underlying fear since perhaps that fear would have made me safer. I do not agree that expecting healthcare workers to live in a constant state of fear and concern for their personal safety is necessarily the strongest foundation for a sound healthcare environment.

Healthcare is a violent arena, as I have mentioned before.

Not only do we struggle with incivility occurring amongst colleagues and co-workers, but we also suffer with violence directed towards us by our clients and patients. As I look back on what I have written, I see the never-ending loop of violence and aggression, growing larger and more vicious, not unlike how a tornado gathers speed and size. I maintain that workplace violence is being allowed not only to continue gaining momentum, but also to elevate the levels of damage it leaves in its wake.

How do we rein this violent culture in and go back to supporting a healing, therapeutic environment? First, we need to take a step back and conduct an honest inventory of ourselves and how violence impacts us, our practice, and our patients. Without this first step, I believe that it will be impossible to move forward and make progress in how it is addressed in our workplaces. As long as there is not an accurate understanding of healthcare workplace violence, it will be difficult to collect data reflecting its presence. Without data, it will continue to thrive and grow in the healthcare industry. After all, if it is not a critical issue, why would the industry choose to spend resources to prevent it, or commit to supporting their employees who are the survivors of it?

We have a right to practice in a safe environment. Our patients and clients have a right to be in a safe and secure place while receiving our care. Until we acknowledge that the presence and acceptance of violence is a common occurrence, we can do little or nothing to prevent, mitigate, and support healing from its damaging effects.

Bullet Journal #7

A legacy is something from the past, carried on into the future. After reading this chapter, take a moment to reflect on your values, beliefs, behaviors, and ideas about the topic of violence in the healthcare workplace. Perhaps do a little research of your own too.

Picture yourself retired, sitting on the porch of your home, and reflecting on your life. What would you like your personal legacy regarding the issue of healthcare workplace violence to be? What changes would you like to be remembered for? Write a sentence for each.

•

•

•

Chapter 8:

Tina Suckow

"They think that I am the person that I was; I know that I'm not."
Tina Suckow, after being assaulted in her workplace

When Tina and I spoke, I was immediately taken with her smile and openness. I offered that she could decide a name of her choosing rather than having her real name in this book; some folks worry about speaking their truth for fear of retribution from their employers, and it's a real fear.

Tina chose to allow the use of her own name, first and last.

That's quite bold, I thought to myself. I confirmed that she really meant that it was going to be okay to see her name in print; it is certainly not my goal to cause chaos and upset in the lives of people who have already been battered in the workplace. Tina replied, "I want people to know my story." And, as Tina saw it, it could only really be her story if her name was attached to it. As I said, it's brave.

My goal in writing the personal stories of the victims of healthcare workplace violence is to put a narrative alongside a statistic. As I said at the beginning, it's about seeing the souls behind the numbers.

Numbers and percentages are so very clinical. It is so much easier to pass by a statistic and assume that it has little to do with us or our lives, just a little blip that popped up in the newsfeed on the smartphone. A real person, complete with a history, family, passions, and goals adds dimension to the statistics. This literal fleshing out of those one-dimensional numbers may cause some true discomfort. When you read Tina's story, I suggest that you approach it with compassion as well as self-compassion. It is difficult to hear the grief, sadness, and struggles. I recommend you focus on Tina and not the assault. She deserves to be defined not by what has been inflicted on her, but by who she was before the assault and who she is now as she works to find her place in a new and unfamiliar world.

I inquired what had inspired Tina to pursue a career in nursing. The response received was lovely in its simplicity. "It is all I ever wanted to do." Tina was the first person in her family to pursue nursing as a vocation. She loved everything about her chosen profession, she said, and when asked what "everything" involved, she answered with a laugh, "Sounds, smells, scrubs, the medical side of nursing, and just feeling competent to help people."

Tina also had an immediate response to the query of how she defined herself.

"Nurse would be the first thing that I would say I am."

The position she held when she was assaulted put her on the frontlines of providing care for the set of patients whom many would consider the 'undesirables'—elderly male sex offenders. Tina has confidently, compassionately, and competently cared for this population.

Her family and friends have known forever that they can call on

Tina when the going gets tough. After all, that's what nurses do, right? They care for people who need them, regardless of how messy the situation is. And she has loved being able to do this.

Tina is the mother of adult children, and is also a grandmother. Accompanying those important life roles is a sense of protectiveness for those around her; this mama bear is used to stepping in and taking care of others, including her co-workers.

I need to acknowledge the assault that occurred while Tina was on duty at the psychiatric hospital where she was employed. There's a great expression that I have often heard when people discuss the outcome of situations caught in a freefall; "hard telling, not knowing." This expression sums up the cascade of events that have ultimately ended the career Tina loved.

The shift started out peacefully enough. The area where Tina was assigned had two staff members on duty that evening. When the call went out from a neighboring unit that needed help to resolve a situation that was becoming increasingly dangerous, Tina responded. What started out as a routine emergency code to provide support to de-escalate the situation and re-establish a safe environment for patients and staff, rapidly changed into every bit of the terrifying nightmare the staff had hoped to avoid.

The patient became increasingly aggressive and mercurial, and in the midst of containing the situation, he made a swift and unexpected turn toward Tina. New and unfamiliar emergency equipment was called into play to aid in controlling the patient. Tina found herself at the bottom of the heap made up of patient, staff, and equipment – not unlike a rugby player at the bottom of the scrum.

When extricated, Tina was left with multiple injuries that would require surgical interventions, along with a serious concussion.

I asked if she was transported by ambulance to the Emergency Department. The immediate response was, "No, I had to ask a co-worker for a ride to the employee health clinic."

I inquired what support Tina received from her workplace. "In the beginning, my co-workers were good about checking in, but that has all pretty much faded away now." Life goes on and it is hard to stay in touch from the sidelines.

What about support from management and the administration of the facility? From the first moments after the assault right through to the bitter end when she was terminated from her position, Tina was assigned blame for her injuries. Little support was offered and, actually, management worked aggressively throwing up roadblocks, which served to make the healing process more difficult. Tina still doesn't understand how this happens. The employer does hold all of the winning cards in the game, though. Tina, unable to return to work, launched into a tailspin of financial challenges such as receiving notification that her family had been dropped from her employer's health insurance plan. Tina's retirement savings have been exhausted to pay for living expenses. And, the bitterest pill of all to swallow? There is no clear picture for Tina of any kind of a future in nursing.

We also discussed how it feels to have an important component of her personal identity taken away so mercilessly. What is it like to be abandoned after spending a career engaged in and part of a profession that cares for people? It feels much like when a ship finds itself without an anchor during a bad storm—lost, battered, and discarded with no clear sense of direction or what the future holds.

Tina has been diagnosed with Post-Traumatic Stress Disorder (PTSD). I asked her what this feels like and how it has changed her life. She finds that it takes an enormous amount of energy to figure out how to manage herself in what used to be very run-of-the-mill situations. An aura of anxiety around the unpredictability of the world dulls her sense of safety. She now lacks the feeling of confidence that had allowed her to move freely and productively in the world before she was assaulted.

Family activities have been down-sized, as Tina avoids attending any function that involves noise, lights, loud noises, or crowds of people. Attending games or other events to see her grandchildren in action is off the table. When a stimulus upsets the delicate balance in this current situation, Tina realizes that she feels stuck in the fight-or-flight mode. She finds that she often has no control over her response and may have an extreme reaction, which doesn't at all fit the situation. As Tina said, "I'm never sure when I am going to break down and start crying… how do you explain that?"

Tina's husband has assumed a new role in their family; that of being Tina's advocate. He is quick to remind friends and family that there are some activities and behaviors that just aren't compatible with keeping Tina's life manageable. As Tina put it, "I'm still learning who I am now, every day." While Tina is grateful for his support, it only confirms to her that her role in their family has shifted from being the protector to being the protected. "All of a sudden, I seemed to become old and fragile," Tina said with a tinge of sadness.

In doing my due diligence before we spoke, I found that Tina had found her voice regarding the issue of healthcare workplace violence. Her story came to the attention of U.S. Rep. Finkenauer (D-Iowa) who has co-sponsored a bill (HR 1309) addressing healthcare workplace violence. I was interested in ferreting out how Tina's story ended up being shared in the U.S. House of Representatives.

Tina was approached by leadership members of the labor union that represented her and asked if they might share her story with Rep. Finkenauer. In the early days, Tina agreed to this as long as her name was not included. She had hoped to return to work and did not want to jeopardize her relationship with her employer by publicly acknowledging where the assault had occurred. The day that Tina's FMLA ran out, she had not yet been medically cleared to return to work; that was the day that she was terminated from her position by her employer. Just like that. Tina had a little epiphany that day; with nothing left to lose, she offered that her whole name could be used moving forward. Tina had found her voice.

Since being terminated from her job, Tina has continued to speak out on the topic of healthcare workplace violence, finding healing through supporting other healthcare workers who have been similarly impacted. Tina has become one of the moderators for the Facebook page, #SilentNoMore, and is very proud of her role. "If we can help someone else going through the nightmare of violence in the workplace, we will have done something worthwhile."

I wondered what Tina sees in her future.

Her dream, she said, is to return to working in nursing since she misses caring for patients. There is a spark of hope that this will work out in spite of the emotional scars and physical challenges remaining from the assault. But for now, "It feels like the world is just going on without me," Tina said in a very small, quiet voice.

Chapter 9:

Trauma and PTSD

Let's start by taking a quick look at the concept of trauma. A traumatic event is an incident that causes physical, emotional, spiritual, or psychological harm. The results of this distressing experience may cause the person who has lived through it to feel threatened, anxious, or frightened as a result. In some cases, they may not know how to respond to the situation and its aftermath. There may even be denial about the effect that the traumatic experience has had on the victim.

Without much effort, we can all think of events that we, or those around us, have experienced which could be considered traumatic. Precipitous childbirth, combat, car accident, rape, physical assault, street violence, medical procedure, or natural disaster are just a few potentially traumatic events. Struggling emotionally after a traumatic event is not uncommon. If adequate resources and support exist for the trauma victim, further sequelae may be minimized. Others who do not have the opportunity, resources and support to heal, may find themselves struggling into the future. It is key to remember that not everyone responds to traumatic events in the same way. There is no gold standard to enforce for how to measure a response to a trauma. You may respond quite differently than the person sitting next to you.

When I was a little girl, there were no malls or online shopping options. Stores downtown were open late on Thursdays because that was payday for many of the factories and mills. It was simple business sense; make sure that the doors of the shops are open while there is a fresh supply of money jingling in pockets of consumers. Woolworth's and Newberry's were two of the shopping temples which were beyond magical in my little girl mind. So many wonderful bits, bobs, and pieces… truly, something for everyone at such very affordable prices. Oh, and the luncheonette at Newberry's with its long, shiny counter complete with stools that spun around and around was an epicurean dream for a meal. I felt that it had only the finest cuisine—French fries, hot dogs, grilled cheese sandwiches made with orange cheese, ice cream–nothing but the best! What a funny word, "luncheonette!"

Another treasure trove was tucked away on a side street. Kelley's Army & Navy sold all sorts of military surplus items. There was so much stuff jammed in there that moving about to search for an item required strategy and cunning. My father used to joke that there was enough gear in there to easily supply a battalion. I guessed that that meant there really was a lot of stuff in that little place. It was much easier when on a shopping mission to just ask the owner, Beulah, to locate the target and bring it to you. Navigating the store also required skirting tactfully around Moe, Beulah's husband. Moe could be found perched on a camp stool, staring straight ahead. If you spoke directly to Moe, he responded with answers consisting of just one word. His affect was flat – totally flat. Moe just was and took up very little actual space.

I began a real love affair with Kelley's Army & Navy when I started high school. The best turtleneck shirts—not only compliant with parochial school dress code, but also priced just right for a girl on a very slim budget—could be found in plentiful supply there. Try as I might, Moe never was up for much of a chat. Curious, I asked my father what Moe's story was.

Poor Moe; he seemed more than a little off to me. I was told that Moe had served in WWII, and before Moe went off to war, he had been just a regular guy. This different Moe was how he had been since he'd returned home. Dad called it battle fatigue. My grandfather, a veteran of the trenches of WWI Battle of Ypres, would have called it shell shock. I don't know where Moe served or what he experienced, but as a nurse and someone interested in the history of medicine, I have wondered what, if any, treatment Moe may have experienced for the symptoms of his so-called battle fatigue.

Nurses have had a long history of showing up where they were needed; especially in wars. They are often in positions where, while caring for patients, they are exposed to life-altering trauma. Dorothy Still was a nurse who served in the U.S. Navy during WWII. She and her colleagues, known as the Sacred Eleven, were captured by the Japanese military.

These nurses spent more than three years providing care to the other prisoners in the prisoner of war (POW) camp where they were incarcerated. Upon returning home, Dorothy struggled. She had seen and lived through horrors that haunted her. At times, she found herself crying for no apparent reason and seemed unable to stop the flow of tears. The Navy psychiatrist's response to Dorothy's concerns was shockingly cruel, seemingly perpetuating the trauma initiated by the war and continued in the POW camp. He told her that she was being ridiculous… nurses could not possibly have the same response to war that soldiers did.

The good news is that Dorothy Still was far more fortunate in her treatment than another WWII Navy nurse, Dorothy Ludden. Dorothy experienced a decline in her mental health culminating in what was known as a nervous breakdown while serving in the U.S. Navy. She was one of 2,000 WWII veterans who received lobotomies through the Veteran's Administration, as treatment for their war-related mental conditions.

Post-Traumatic Stress Disorder (PTSD) is the name currently accepted to describe symptoms and sequelae associated with the aftermath of a traumatic experience. This newer name encompasses more than just battlefield trauma. Psychiatry has come a long way in acknowledging PTSD causes, aftermath, and treatment options. The Diagnostic and Statistical Manual (DSM-5) is the psychiatric professions' official manual of mental health disorders. Simply stated, based on the criteria in the DSM-5, PTSD occurs after a person has experienced a traumatic event, most usually involving or threatening death, significant injury, or sexual violence. This experience may be first-hand, be witnessed happening to someone else, or happen to a loved one. Hearing the graphic details of a violent event over and over may also cause PTSD. The general symptoms of PTSD include intrusive memories, nightmares, overwhelming feelings of stress when reminded of the event, and flashbacks when triggered by reminders of what was experienced. The three categories of PTSD symptoms are: arousal and reactivity, avoidance, and cognition. For a diagnosis of PTSD to be made, one has to exhibit a certain number of symptoms in each of these categories, each of these lasting longer than a month.

Another piece of the diagnostic criteria requires that the presence of these symptoms interfere with personal relationships and work responsibilities. PTSD, undiagnosed and untreated, stands to have a negative impact on both work and personal relationships, carrying an increased risk of dying by suicide.

Safe to say, pretending that trauma has not had an impact or that the symptoms of PTSD don't really exist, only sets up a cascade of downward-spiraling feelings and behaviors making life far more challenging and joyless.

Like the pre-war version of Moe, many healthcare workers start out bright-eyed and bushy tailed, but PTSD may be acquired through trauma experienced in the workplace.

Some advocate for updating the name to Post Traumatic Stress Injury and dropping the word "disorder," theoretically decreasing the stigma associated with having a psychiatric disorder diagnosis. After all, these symptoms are caused by events over which the victim had no control, which have directly impacted unwilling participants–the after-effects of an injury.

There is little or no mystery that vicariously experiencing a patient's disaster may have a lasting impact on the caregiver. Think about the Emergency Department team working doggedly to save a small child caught in a drive-by shooting. How does this remotely make any sense? What compartment can that experience be tucked into? How many similar events will happen in the future? How vulnerable is the caregiver's family to life-threatening disaster? Over time, what toll do these situations exact on the healers?

Similarly, direct violence has an impact on healthcare workers. Healthcare facilities are staffed around the clock, every day of the year, with many dedicated, compassionate folks. There is a stalwart determination to aid, comfort, and heal. There are many in healthcare who very much take this intention quite seriously. So, it's somewhat hard to imagine that anybody goes into the patient care arena with the understanding that they may very well be physically and emotionally battered with a DSM-5 psychiatric diagnosis as a result. What happens when the caregiver is the target of the violence, then—when they are harmed by the very people for whom they have pledged to care? I should warn you, statistics are a valuable tool, but not necessarily accurate. In terms of healthcare and job-related PTSD associated with it, the system is organized in such a way that under-reporting of the symptoms that would diagnose PTSD is almost to be expected. Once again, surveys done by professional organizations give us a small view of the prevalence as experienced by those working in healthcare.

Remember that old story about 'stone soup'? The one where the soldiers arrived in a town and found that the locals were unwilling to share their surplus with hungry strangers? So, the soldiers cunningly devised a plan to trick the villagers. The travelers declared that they had a magical stone which, when simply boiled in a pot of water, would make the most marvelous soup ever consumed. While skeptical, the locals were still intrigued. Of course, if the villagers were to each contribute a little bit of produce or meat, the soup would be that much more magnificent and there would be enough to share with the whole village. As each citizen delivered their contribution to the soup kettle, the end product became more and more tantalizing. Everyone had plenty to eat and they all lived happily ever after.

You may be pondering how this story applies to a healthcare facility and PTSD caused by workplace events. Fair enough. Imagine that a hospital is rather like a kettle full of water and the healthcare workers plus medical resources are the magical stone placed in it. The patients and visitors bring needs and concerns that end up providing the substance of this medical stew. Some of these seasonings consist of, but are not limited to: fatal injuries, serious domestic or child abuse, psychiatric illness, and violence perpetrated against healthcare workers. It is not surprising that facing this horror on a regular basis can result in a soup made bitter with PTSD.

There is little data that has been generated regarding the rate of PTSD in healthcare workers, but what I located sounded a warning. The American College of Emergency Physicians (ACEP) is a group that has dipped a toe into the turbulent waters of PTSD and its effects on physicians. The emergency department provides a fertile environment in which to gain exposure to a perfect storm of stressors that can result in PTSD. Anyone who has had the misfortune to spend even a small amount of time in the churning chaos of the ED knows that people often arrive in that place on the worst day of their lives. Or, because they have no regular access to healthcare. Or, they have been the victim of their own or another's bad choice. Or, because they are struggling and there is no other place to take them. Or, because that department never, ever closes.

What about those statistics? Surveys, once again, are the source of the numbers. Roughly 15-17% of emergency medicine physicians and 18% of nurses meet the diagnostic criteria of PTSD. Emergency medicine residents demonstrate increasing rates of PTSD with each year of residency. There are estimates that by the end of residency, the rate of PTSD may be as high as 30%. There are large areas of healthcare that have not been surveyed or studied regarding the prevalence of PTSD.

The term PTSD has become part of our everyday language. It is common to hear folks casually mention that they were triggered by some event or behavior. It is safe to say that it is a rare person in our world who has not experienced some sort of trauma, but not all trauma leads to the diagnosis of PTSD. Being triggered by a reminder of the traumatic event for someone with PTSD can be a very different experience than for someone who has not met the criteria for that diagnosis.

How do triggers work? In my personal experience, a trigger is a stimulus in the current environment, which immediately immerses me in the sense of being back in the middle of the assault. It is both physical and emotional in nature. My response is an uncontrollable knee jerk reaction that, to anyone who doesn't understand the background, seems totally illogical. I am vigilant and mindful regarding my surroundings in order to maintain some sense of control and avoid potential disasters.

Recently, I was sent for a magnetic resonance imaging scan (MRI) of my neck. It was during the pandemic, so masks were required in the MRI suite. To keep the number of people in the building to a minimum, nobody was allowed to accompany me. The technicians had a schedule to follow so the two of them were diligently attending to tasks simultaneously to get the scan underway.

Noisy room, ear plugs put in early, unable to see faces or hear instructions, dark and very small area, two people touching me without warning, and having my head restrained all served to ramp up my sense of panic. Pulse racing, sweating, and nauseated, I soldiered on. Then, suddenly, the whole machine started moving me into the 'tube.' I hit a level of panic response that impressed all of us. I literally clawed my way out of the tube, screaming.

Looking back without judgment, I understand that that experience triggered a response that may have seemed quite extreme to those around me. I was helpless, restrained. People were touching me without warning, and then the final blow came when it felt like I was being put in a coffin while still alive. I was acutely aware of being very alone in the machine. Many of the triggers I experienced are linked directly to the assault I had suffered. Regaining consciousness on the floor after the assault with nobody to explain what had happened or to reassure me had set the stage for events, such as the MRI, to require a great deal of preparation and skill—both for me and those doing the examination.

It's helpful to take a look at the symptoms that must be present in order to make the diagnosis of the PTSD. Here is the broad overview:

PTSD is characterized by three main types of symptoms. The first group of symptoms includes: flashbacks, nightmares, and intrusive memories of the traumatic event. The next group of symptoms encompasses emotional numbness and avoidance of places, people, and activities that are reminders of the trauma. The final group of symptoms consists of behaviors associated with increased arousal: difficulty sleeping and concentrating, feeling "nervous" and jumpy, and being easily angered and irritated. PTSD is diagnosed after symptoms are experienced for at least one month following a traumatic event. However, symptoms may not appear until several months or even years later.

I have struggled to write this chapter, and I am challenged daily to live with the effects of PTSD. Yes, indeed, I now sport a DSM-5 psychiatric diagnosis. I find it a frightening undertaking, at times, to navigate life and establish a bit of order. Some days are more of an adventure than others. What once didn't require any planning or preparation, now causes almost unbearable anxiety.

Please don't ask me to join in with a spur of the moment activity; I will always decline the offer. I now require time to wrap my head around the plan and fabricate an exit strategy in case I need to leave. I was confident, in control, always considered to be the problem solver, working two jobs, and perpetually looking forward to the future. Now, however, there are times when I just can't wait for the day to come to an end.

Crowds are hard to be around because I just cannot survey around me enough to be sure there will be no potentially unsafe behavior. To make matters worse, since we started wearing masks during the COVID-19 pandemic, reading faces has become an almost impossible chore. Anything moving quickly toward me, loud noises, or people touching me unexpectedly sets off a predictable cascade of physical fight, flight, or freeze responses, any or all of which may be interpreted by others as being hard to get along with. In addition to all of this, I am regularly visited by horrible nightmares, all so lifelike that I sometimes become confused whether they happen in what passes for sleep, or if they were real.

Social isolation has become my norm. I like to have control over my surroundings; I've learned that loud noises, especially shouting, are panic inducing. I used to enjoy being around people, but now I find myself irritated by and angry at seemingly silly things. I literally have learned to bite my tongue, turn around, and walk briskly away to avoid lashing out. Days can be lonely and joyless. I am so ashamed that this is my life; after all, I am supposed to be the dependable one, the person folks can count on in a pinch; creative, kind, fearless, and always ready to listen to the problems of others. Some days, I am not terribly sure of who I am anymore.

Making my way through this maze requires thoughtfulness, self-compassion, and boundaries; it's all a lot of hard work.

A couple of months after I was assaulted, I was walking my two Shih Tzus, Henry and Barnaby. Suddenly, seemingly from out of nowhere, two large dogs came racing toward us snarling and barking, hell bent on having their fun with my little leashed pups. That day, I learned something about my new self. Those two dogs, a German Shepherd and a pit bull mix, aggressively attacked my terrified little dogs as I tried to pick them up out of harm's way.

The aggressors were having none of it and started to bite me to get to my little guys. We were outgunned, outweighed, and it appeared to be a hopeless situation. I had a flash of a thought that I was going to watch Barnaby and Henry be killed as I held onto the other end of their leashes. In that moment, I became someone I had never met before, fighting like a wild woman with my hands and feet to protect my dogs. I can honestly say that I could have killed the aggressors, or died trying, if the owner had not finally made an appearance and attempted to catch them.

There was no on/off switch or thought for my own safety, just the response to fight—if necessary, to the death. When all was said and done, I was the only one who had scars from being bitten and the little dogs were safe.

In the time since the workplace assault, I have learned to acknowledge my feelings and try to find a safe place in the world. Relationships with friends and family have shifted. Things are not what they were, but with effort and mindfulness, I am carving out space to honor the new me. Some days are definitely better than others, and I can now say the assault and aftermath no longer define me—only a part of me. I allow myself to still grieve what has been lost.

What helps to manage PTSD? Simple things assist a great deal, such as being able to candidly discuss the feelings associated with the traumatic experience; having access to a social system that actively supports working through the trauma is far more helpful to promote healing than isolation. Also, having the support of a circle of friends and family who are constantly engaged and non-judgmental can help the survivor of violence to gain a sense of perspective about the trauma.

I also found that, with the help of a counselor, revising my perspective and giving myself credit for realigning my beliefs have been key in shifting my thinking about my PTSD symptoms. Daily, I push away feelings of shame and blame, working hard to respect my own boundaries and manage my response to situations. I also give myself credit now for being a survivor, rather than being ashamed of being a victim of the assault. While I am not the same person I was before, I have survived, and this book has allowed me to find my voice and given meaning to a traumatic situation… one that I never expected to form a part of my nursing career.

In retrospect, I wonder what could have been done so that healing could have been promoted from the very beginning of my journey. Perhaps my life would be different now. Due to the common workplace culture of assigning blame and shame to those healthcare workers who have had the great misfortune to be assaulted, it has become evident that isolating is quick to be instituted by most workplaces. Out of sight, out of mind—and the show can go on. Shaming victims is an easy route to take to package up the responsibility for the injuries. It is much easier to question an injured individual's professional judgment and competency than to focus on any institutional accountability or responsibility.

The workplace is then rendered safe from becoming the focus of any attention that may result in an inspection of its policies and procedures regarding employee safety.

But the human cost of discarding assaulted employees is not only a burden for the survivor, but for the whole healthcare system. Although disposing of a worker is far more streamlined for the industry than solving the systemic issues that allowed the violence to occur, we really cannot afford to throw away our dedicated healthcare workers. For many, the post-assault emotional support and psychiatric care are hit or miss offerings. Programs may exist to fulfill the letter of the law and look great on paper, but when an employee is the victim of a serious assault, the programs may lack the depth of intervention and qualifications to meet the needs of the employee and any witnesses of the assault.

For example, what if someone had stepped up and called an ambulance for me, rather than expecting me to triage my injuries and make that decision? And if perhaps the staff at the local hospital would have taken the time to actually survey all of my physical injuries, would it have changed the course of how the assault impacted my life? Another thought: what if my fears for my safety had been acknowledged and reassurance given to me?

Would my outcome have changed if I'd had an advocate alongside me when I was dropped in front of the hospital door? And if someone had taken the time to call my children who were listed as the emergency contacts on my personnel forms, would the severity of my situation have been recognized? Would the offer of support early on have made a difference in the long run?

Would the longer-term emotional outcome have been different if a counselor had come to see me while I was still in the hospital, when the wounds both physical and mental were still fresh and I desperately required a listening ear to unburden myself of everything?

If someone had explained to me what had actually happened during the continuing assault while I lay unconscious—rather than letting me try to figure it out based on my bruises, or waiting until the police showed up the next morning to investigate—what difference would that have made?

What if I hadn't had to negotiate for every single little piece of care I received through Worker's Compensation?

What if fellow employees and management were encouraged to show up at the hospital to be at my side, metaphorically and literally, and if someone in management had apologized, saying (and meaning it) that they were so, so sorry that this had happened to me?

What if the charge nurse hadn't later chastised me for not having completed my charting before going to the hospital, thus causing the rest of the staff, traumatized by watching the assault, to be burdened by having to finish my work?

So many "what ifs" exist in this story.

One of the best gifts that we can give ourselves in this kind of scenario is to learn from history, so that experiences resembling mine are handled differently.

That is a big part of my goal in writing this book.

Let's just take a moment to really unpack this messy business of PTSD and how it may impact a healthcare worker.

PTSD is classified as a psychiatric disorder occurring after a traumatic event; an episode which, for many healthcare workers, happens within their workplace. Treatments and medications are available that could possibly help to alleviate suffering. But strangely enough, in many states, a licensed professional must report psychiatric diagnoses and treatments to their licensing bodies, which then have the power to demand oversight of the treatment and, in some cases, deny licensure. This method of forcing the healthcare professional to 'admit' to receiving treatment for a psychiatric issue as part of the licensure process is fraught with potential for negative outcomes. At the least, it sets up a lose-lose situation for the struggling healthcare professionals and their patients. Healthcare providers find that seeking access for needed emotional support is inhibited by this arrangement. At the worst, it punishes healthcare providers for seeking help by taking away the opportunity to work in their profession. So, the disorder, which often has its roots in the workplace, may have to be ignored and allowed to fester through neglect and lack of care.

How, then, can we best support a struggling coworker in this situation? Medicine and nursing fall prey to a warrior mentality… buck up, put it out of your mind, and move on to the next battle. It seems as though the present system is not only hiding the problem of PTSD, but also slamming the door shut on its effective treatment. And the warriors are getting tired of it.

A perfect storm is brewing, I think.

After perusing the literature, I can honestly say that very little is organized or offered for healthcare workers who are injured during violence in the workplace, although some programs do exist to provide peer support after a troubling incident—a sort of psychological first aid.

An interesting conundrum is found in the example of one of the biggest proponents of safety in healthcare, Johns Hopkins Hospital. Recently, this hospital found itself put forward for a place on the "Dirty Dozen" Employers list organized by the Council for Occupational Safety and Health 2019.

The winners of the "Dirty Dozen" have the dubious distinction of putting workers and communities at risk due to their unsafe practices. Johns Hopkins Hospital won their place on this list with the statistic that four-fifths of their nursing staff report that they have been victims of workplace violence. Sadly, 25% of the nurses go on to say that the organization ignores these dangers. It will bear watching to see if there is any kind of organizational change in the making to prevent violence and address the needs of victims after being publicly outed on this list.

Anecdotally, some have found help through their workplace's Employee Assistance Program (EAP), but not all EAP offices have staff trained to work with clients who have suffered workplace trauma or are experiencing symptoms of PTSD. It is, as always, important to evaluate the scope of practice of a service, and not make assumptions about what it has to offer.

Assaulted Staff Action Programs (ASAP) also exist in some facilities, their goal being to provide support to staff who have just experienced workplace violence; ASAP responders include staff and management. Like many good ideas and well-developed plans that meet the gold standard of an industry, opportunities abound for haphazard implementation and follow-through. Indeed, some employees may be reticent about using a service where the waters of confidentiality may be muddied by communicating concerns with a member of management who is acting in the role of a peer counselor. It should also be noted that it is key for any program to know its limits, based on skills/knowledge, the severity of the incident, or symptoms exhibited.

Cleveland Clinic Hospitals have started a program known as "Code Lavender." A Code Lavender is initiated when challenging situations threaten unit stability, personal emotional equilibrium, or professional functioning. Code Lavender utilizes evidence-based relaxation and restoration interventions to help people during the crisis. This measure provides staff with support to enable them to cope with and make sense out of the challenging situation at hand with the goal of letting more permanent solutions emerge in the future.

When a Code Lavender is called, there is a response to the affected area within thirty minutes, and the responders are not there to fulfill the needs of the institution, but those of the staff members.

I did also find a little glimmer of hope (wait for it…) in my search for help with PTSD.

Project Hope: EMS is an organization started by and geared toward supporting emergency medical technicians (EMT) and paramedics struggling with PTSD. Pre-hospital care is a dangerous undertaking in the best of situations. Add in the myriad of violent influences and it is not surprising that many EMTs and paramedics are tasked to deliver care in terrifying situations.

Patients and families often lash out with both verbal and physical abuse. Multiply this by the injury, death, and destruction that take up whole shifts, and the pressure cooker rapidly reaches critical levels of steam, a hefty burden to drag around. When I looked at the Project Hope page, an image quickly caught my attention; this group is lobbying to have the name changed from PTSD to Post-Traumatic Stress Injury. After all, it was not a disorder that healthcare workers were born with, but rather an injury that they acquired in the workplace.

While nomenclature of medical diagnoses is not under the purview of the frontline workers in healthcare, the distinction made in this description does feel important. Does rebranding a disorder into an injury shift the burden of stigma as we invest energy in salvaging healthcare workers? Will it open the door for access to services and support?

It seems surprising how little traction has been gained for even gathering the data which would begin the process of acknowledging the saber-toothed tiger in the room—violence in the healthcare workplace with accompanying PTSD.

I get it. Thinking about your doctor or nurse being beaten or verbally abused is not a glowing public relations opportunity for the healthcare industry. My father's classic expression, 'out of sight, out of mind' has served the healthcare industry well. Unfortunately, violence in the healthcare workplace is a brutal reality impacting each and every facet of healthcare.

What is the first step to take to start healing? Looking at the saber-toothed tiger of violence and the resulting PTSD in healthcare is key. It exists; it leaves a mark. And that mark, if we don't address it, can cause damage.

Time to air healthcare's dirty laundry. Pretending that workplace violence against health workers or soul-sucking patient care are not problems but just constitute "a part of the job" is to do an enormous disservice to both staff and patients.

I would go so far as to assert that it becomes an issue of the sustainability of healthcare services.

The second step might just be to follow in the footsteps of the first responders, and to start taking care of ourselves and each other. If we are willing to acknowledge the scope and impact of violence in healthcare, we can move on to actively working to care for ourselves and each other. If there's no problem, then we don't need a solution, right? Time to drag those ostriches' heads out of their handy holes in the ground. I believe that we will gain strength and momentum to create positive healing environments only after we take that first step of admitting to ourselves and each other that healthcare workers have been and are being broken by healthcare workplace violence.

Important Take-Aways

- PTSD may not be "cured." For many, it takes boatloads of hard work to learn to manage it.
- Distance yourself from the judgment of those who have no understanding of your work or experiences. When you are feeling vulnerable, it is far too easy to take someone's harsh criticism or intrusive question to heart—possibly, with damaging consequences.
- Understand that people may say incredibly unhelpful things; this is their ignorance speaking. They have not stood where you stand, and almost certainly just don't

grasp what happened to you and how you feel or struggle as a result.

- Also, understand that people's opinions about the healthcare industry may very well not reflect your reality.
- Lectures to "get a grip" or, my favorite, "keep a song in your heart" aren't helpful. Don't feel that you need to listen to them. You are also not obligated to give them.
- Give yourself permission to NOT accept blame or shame directed toward you about the assault.
- For those who appreciate visual demonstrations, this is what PTSD looks like: locate a fresh piece of paper... all smooth and clean. Proceed to crumple the paper up into a tight ball, and finally, flatten the sheet of paper and try to get it back into its original form. Are you able to make it go back to what it was before you crumpled it? That is a visual of what PTSD feels like... still a piece of paper, but forever crinkled and unable to return to the pristine form.
- Think about what you use for coping mechanisms. How do they help you?
- Know yourself. Know what triggers your feelings of anxiety and/or depression. Practice self-nourishing, especially when helping a colleague who may be struggling after a traumatic event.
- Honor your needs. You do not have to explain how PTSD feels personally, or to justify having it, or to answer questions.
- It is not your job to rationalize or explain your feelings to people. You do not have to share your story if you don't want to... It is your story to tell or to keep to yourself.
- Ignoring uncomfortable feelings does not make them go away.
- Asking for help is a sign of strength.

For those supporting colleagues or loved ones who are healing after a traumatic event:

- Verbalize that you will be there for the person who is struggling but you will not impose.
- Do concrete activities to show support: send a note, bring a meal to share, offer transportation, and company for appointments.
- Resist the urge to organize or control their recovery. Being assaulted is one form of control; they do not also need to be told exactly what they need to do to recover. If they want to sleep, they can sleep. If they want a cigarette, they can smoke. They do not need to be told when to bathe, take a walk, or talk about things. Don't smother. Just be on hand.
- Make clear that you are willing to just be present. If they want to talk or be silent, it is their choice. Be willing to stay if they need your presence during the hardest times. But when they expressly wish you to leave them alone, do it without taking offense.
- Let them understand that they are not expected to explain or discuss anything, and that you are simply available for whatever is useful to them.
- State clearly that this situation is not fair; the victim is in no way responsible for what happened to them.
- Validate the victim's feelings, don't try to talk them out of how they are feeling. And don't tell them other people's anecdotes—or your own. They have enough of a trauma story already.
- Respect boundaries. This means only talking to the victim about their situation, and not talking about them with others—not even their friends and family who have

also shown up to support them. It may also mean not encouraging/shaming the victim to do anything that is out of their comfort zone.

- Understand that everyone's response to a traumatic event is different. There is no 'one size fits all' for how to feel or how to deal with after-effects.

Bullet Journal #8

Take a deep breath. Let it all out and take another. Being a witness to or a part of traumatic events is challenging; no matter how much energy goes into preparing for them, the experience can take up space in your heart and soul. I have written this portion of your bullet journal to provide you with the space to do the brave work of making an inventory of your thoughts and ideas around these sorts of experiences.

You will have heard about triggers that can cause a sudden shift in your sympathetic nervous response (fight/flight/freeze) to situations. Give yourself permission to sit down and think about this concept. What are some situations you find challenging?

•

•

•

What are some of your coping mechanisms when you have had an emotionally challenging experience and are trying to process it and gain a sense of equilibrium? No need to judge these coping mechanisms as good or bad. Just identify what they are.

•

•

•

What emotional support do you need in order to do your chosen work and maintain your own health?

-
-
-

What do you see yourself offering to others who are struggling with difficult situations?

-
-
-

Chapter 10:

Oh, the Difference a Day Can Make...

When I was young and enthusiastic, I graduated from college with a degree in social work. My intention was to find a position as a caseworker in a freestanding hospice. How we treated people who were at the end of life was changing in wonderful ways, and I felt strongly that I wanted to be a part of this evolution in care. Sadly, no sooner had I arrived on the social services scene with my freshly printed diploma than I discovered that political events had shredded the majority of opportunities for entry-level social workers like myself.

Ronald Reagan was the U.S. President and legislative efforts drew heavy lines through entire lists of social service programs, and with them went many human service jobs. My mother had worked for many years in nursing and she had always impressed upon me her firm desire that I never, ever, should consider following in her footsteps. Much to her horror and irritation, that was exactly the next career path that I chose to follow.

Funny how things turn out so differently than what we plan, isn't it? I have never worked in a freestanding hospice nor do I expect that I ever will. The majority of my nursing career has been spent working in the operating room, and I consider it an honor and privilege to have worked with many talented colleagues providing care to patients who have trusted us, literally, with their lives. After spending more than thirty years working in that environment, it was time for me to enjoy a new area of practice.

Finances are often the deciding factor when pursuing further education, and I was certainly no different regarding this consideration; I became a single parent when my children were quite young and, to provide for them, I often worked overtime, took extra call shifts, and worked at a second job. At long last, my youngest child was getting ready to graduate from college. I was finally going to be in the clear to focus on my own career now, rather than just cobbling together resources to balance the family budget.

Life is strange. We get so tangled up with the minutiae of the tasks of daily living that we often don't see where the undercurrent is carrying us or those we love. Work, bills, orthodontic appointments, elderly family members' dwindling capacities, laundry, and the like fill our days. I realize now that there is often no clear picture of the end game while still in the midst of playing it on the field, and my family has been no different.

While I was busy with chores, both of my children blossomed into wonderful adults and have chosen paths that provide care and support to the vulnerable in our world. My son is a physician and my daughter a social worker.

Not long ago, I was sifting through some old stacks of accumulated paperwork. While much of what had been saved and hidden away over the years was clearly bound for the recycling bucket, I did find a little pearl amongst the mess. Tucked inside one of those piles of old bills and appointment reminders was a copy of the first draft of my son's personal statement which he wrote as part of his medical school application process.

It's funny how other people actually see us after all is said and done. I remember worrying that my presence was often lacking at key moments in my children's lives, as I felt I had missed the most important events such as holidays, performances, basketball games, sick days (always a bad day for a nurse when she has to leave her own who need her care in order to meet the needs of her employer), prom photo sessions, and the like. It seemed they were always in conflict with my work and call schedule. At best, I figured that I would go down in their memories as being the definition of an absentee mother. After re-reading the sheet of paper I had discovered in those old documents, I wondered if I may have been too critical of myself.

With my son's permission, I am sharing a portion of that personal statement:

'My first memory is of a hospital. It's not much: bright fluorescent lights that hurt my eyes, shiny floors, strange machines, tall people in bizarre clothes, and a single packet of saltine crackers. I was only two years old at the time; my mother was in labor with my sister, Rachel, and I had been given the lofty task of bringing her a packet of crackers so that she might feel a little better. I had no idea that I was sent on my quest so that I would stop trying to climb up on the bed, as I was squirming dangerously close to the IV and all manner of important equipment. The pair of saltines that I carefully guarded until their delivery did not contain any powerful medicine that would make my mother well again. In fact, I wouldn't be surprised if they were never eaten at all.

'This initial memory is more a blend of emotions and sensations that were ingrained into my mind and then augmented by the various details of the story that I was just too young to remember, but were featured in the account of the night that my mother would later relate to me. It was my first of many memorable experiences I've had in a medical setting. Growing up in a household with a single mother who works long hours as an OR nurse, you learn your way around hospitals. It wasn't unusual that my sister and I would be with her when she was on-call and her pager went off. We spent many long nights in the nurses' lounge watching TV, knowing that there were nurses, technicians, housekeepers, and other members of the OR family there watching out for us. When we were in middle school, my sister and I would do our homework in the hospital library until it was time to go home. I always enjoyed hearing the interesting stories that my mother brought home with her, and I still look forward to hearing about the unusual cases that sometimes come to the OR. Even when I wasn't at the hospital, many of the important people in my young life were medical professionals.

'Given this sort of background, one might think that I was always destined to spend my life in the medical field. Maybe this is true. I was certainly raised in that culture and feel at home within it. If I was always on this trajectory, it took me quite a long time to realize it. I didn't want to be a doctor when I was a child. I wanted to be a paleontologist. I wanted to be a zookeeper. A zoologist. A veterinarian. A helicopter pilot. A Navy Seal. A police officer. Finally, my interests turned toward physical therapy, and then, as a senior in high school, I decided that I wanted to go to medical school…

'…I'm confident that if I use my talents to help other people, if I can make life even a little better for someone else, if I can ensure the dignity of another person in death, then I will go to bed satisfied with my choice of profession at night and I will be satisfied with the life that I have chosen to lead when it finally comes to an end.

'Although I was never pushed toward a profession in medicine, I would be remiss if I didn't give my mother some credit for instilling these values in me. During my senior year of high school, my mother and I spent part of a Saturday looking through ski shops in Lincoln, New Hampshire. On the drive north, she began to cry. She explained that the previous day, she had been part of an especially difficult case. A woman came in for a bowel resection to remove a massive amount of necrotic tissue. The woman was fully conscious and thinking clearly when she came in, but she was also aware that she was likely about to go to sleep for the last time. This patient could never be taken off a ventilator and she died within days of the procedure. My mother apologized for crying and said that after so many years in the OR, she probably shouldn't still cry about these things. I, somewhat matter-of-factly responded that if the day were to come when she stopped caring so much about her patients, she should probably take that as a sign to quit nursing.

'I hope that in my own medical career I will be able to emulate my mother's courage and compassion. It was through her that I learned about patient advocacy. She taught me that it is a healthcare professional's duty first and foremost to always do what is in the best interest of the patient. She taught me that it is an honor to be entrusted with the care of patients who are afraid and at their most vulnerable. She taught me that it is a privilege to care for others at the moment of their death...'

Jonathan, is now a resident physician in a large metropolitan medical center. I sincerely hope that he can hold onto these key pillars for practice while faced with the brutal realities of the healthcare industry today.

Looking back, I realize that a day can make an enormous difference... a major pivot in life, if you will. I have often joked that I plan to work until lunch on the day of my funeral. Dark humor, I know. Part of my plan to be able to meet this goal was taking the time to further my education. With my daughter heading toward her own college graduation, it felt like the right time for me to go back to school and open up some new opportunities. I found a local university offering a bridge program to gain an Advanced Practice Registered Nurse qualification in Psychiatric Mental Health Nursing. This appeared to be an ideal way to blend my original education in social work with my passion for nursing.

Partway through the program, I began to get a little restless. Perhaps it was time to get my boots on the ground and take the leap into psychiatric nursing. Nursing positions were open at a local psychiatric hospital and I felt that it would be prudent to get some experience working in the mental health field. I continued working at my old hospital in the operating room job on weekends, and settled into a staff nurse position on the evening shift at the psychiatric hospital.

On Sunday, June 25, 2017, I worked a per diem shift in the OR at the medical center where I had worked full-time prior to accepting the new position at the psychiatric facility. It was good to maintain my perioperative nursing skills plus having a second income was certainly a benefit for the family budget! It was a great day. I spent time with one of my favorite surgeons doing challenging cases. Our team worked well together and the day was productive and peaceful.

On Monday, June 26, 2017, I was back at the psychiatric facility for my assigned evening shift. The mood of the staff was optimistic and positive. We heard in report that the milieu was calm and upbeat. When it was like that, I always hoped to have the time to sit in the High Visibility Area (HVA) across from the nurses' station and talk with patients. The hand-off report between shifts was usually pretty anecdotal. I struggled with this since I was used to dealing with much more objective hand-offs in the operating room. I found it challenging at times, because I never felt as though I really knew what had transpired with the plans and medication changes on the day shift. It felt as if we were often stuck with the unpleasant responses to these decisions, with little understanding of the rationale behind making them.

Our shift started peacefully enough. One of the patients had "fainted" and was transported to the Emergency Department at the local general hospital to be evaluated. We anticipated that she would be sent back to the psychiatric facility that same evening. I ate my supper early so I would be free to get a transfer report on the patient's status and get her settled back on the unit when she returned.

The nurses all had the chance to eat supper, which was nice, and then we could start charting.

From my experience, a hospital unit is very much like a beehive. As I understand it, seemingly small shifts in the atmosphere can change the entire mood of the hive. The change in mood determines the behaviors that the bees exhibit. The peaceful milieu began to subtly shift to a different, more agitated feel after supper had finished. There was a buzz out in the high-visibility sitting area across from the nurses' station.

Two of the patients had become engaged to marry and the groom-to-be was increasingly territorial regarding his fiancée, his aggressive energy spreading through the rest of the milieu like an invisible toxic gas. A group of male patients had settled in together, sitting not far away in the men's annex. This little cluster felt a bit like an intimidating gang when they were together, with a few of them regaling the others with stories from the past, telling of a time when they had been incarcerated at the State Prison.

Finally, I received word that the patient was being transported back from the local hospital. I was on the fringes of the milieu receiving the report on the patient from a nurse at the local hospital while others were trying to get charting done before the heavy 8 p.m. med pass. Charting was cumbersome and time-consuming. It seemingly took forever to finish hearing the hospital report over the phone and then sorting out transportation to get the patient returned to us.

We were starting to get meds out with constant interruptions for PRN medications. The male patient who was recently engaged came up to me to complain about a mental health worker (MHW) being around his girlfriend. I remember thinking that I was completely befuddled about how this engagement proposal had been handled, because so many boundaries had seemingly been crossed. The whole episode had almost been made into a joke during the report. In my mind, I was questioning why this boyfriend/girlfriend relationship was being validated by management. The groom-to-be had a history of violent behavior so it seemed risky to keep both of the patients in the same unit. After listening to his concerns, he and I negotiated that he would take a break from the milieu. He went to his room, directly across from the male annex, and soon, he returned to the desk. He simply could not let go of his concerns about the MHW and his girlfriend, and no suggestions of coping mechanisms or redirection seemed to help. I wondered if there was anything in the PRN medication category that would assist, or if he would even take a medication, or if it would just make him angrier. He turned and walked back to his room.

By now, the chores were piling up. We were doing the med pass, patients were making requests, the evening snack was about to be offered, and group activities were starting.

A few minutes later, loud banging and men's voices resounded from down the hall as the groom-to-be was literally kicking the door off its hinges with his bare feet. There was a bit of conversation between one of the patients in the annex and the patient who was kicking. The charge nurse and I went part way down the hall and decided that we wouldn't approach the violent patient without plenty of support. In the background, I could hear that the patients in the male annex were laughing and egging him on.

A Code Grey—a psychiatric emergency—was called in order to get more help from other nursing units as I remember thinking to myself that we had very little in our toolbox to manage this dangerous situation. But very few people came in response to the request for assistance, and all the while, this angry patient continued to kick at the door. Now, it was completely off the hinges and he could lift it and use it as a weapon. If it seems not credible that a man would have the power to use a door in such a way, then you need to understand the almost superhuman power and strength that seems to come to some psychiatric patients when they are riled; in fact, we all can do way more than we imagined possible when we are filled with anger and adrenaline.

But this whole situation was also becoming more surreal by the second. We truly had absolutely nothing that could give us the upper hand or to help us safely de-escalate the situation. The charge nurse asked for another Code Grey to be called because she felt that the situation was far too dangerous to manage with only the staff at hand.

I wondered what we might have available in our wheelhouse to protect the staff and patients if no reinforcements arrived to help. Or what would happen if there simply weren't any more staff members in the building… what would happen then? My mind was in overdrive, the blood pumping through my veins, my mind trying to run through all the possible scenarios… the many what ifs.

Thankfully, though, this time, the response to the Code Grey brought more help, including the campus police officer, and we were able to breathe freer—not by much, but at least the cries for help had been heard and heeded, and we had gathered a little more collective strength. It was not yet a sigh of relief, but we felt more supported, anyway. And as we approached the patient's room, I saw that this police officer had his taser out; now, a palpable feeling of a power shift came over us with the addition of more staff. The patient seemed just a little more compliant, perhaps, agreeing to walk to the seclusion room, but all the while still chatting with his homies about what a good fighter he was. They probably remembered seeing him fight in the prison.

Anyway, they continued to sit in the male annex while we went back and tried to salvage the evening routine.

I sat with the patient's so-called girlfriend to assess how she was coping with the events, but oddly, I found her totally disconnected from the violence that had just occurred, and all she wanted was to sit and talk with me about her plans for her upcoming discharge. I remember wondering if she realized how very dangerous this man could be.

I then checked in with the MHW who was the subject of the patient's aggression.

I continued passing out meds and charting; my patient was due back from the hospital at any time. While finishing up the med pass (at least as much as we could), groups were still happening, maintenance took the door away, and an MHW put a blanket up in the doorway for privacy. I was desperately behind in charting, starting to feel as if I was sinking. One of the patients asked me to sit with her and sing to her so that she "could have a happy memory."

In the past, she had consistently refused medication and this was one way to connect with her to encourage her to take her evening meds. I sat and sang, "You are my Sunshine" for about fifteen minutes, and I was happy when she agreed to consider taking her medications.

And now, a whole hour had passed since the psychiatric safety emergency (PSE), and it was time to go into the locked seclusion room to reassess the patient. I was the only female in the group that went into that room, where the patient continued to be aggressive, viewing himself as the victim of the situation. Periodically, he would make abrupt moves toward the males in the group, taunting, cajoling, and testing them all. It felt as though he was going out of his way to manipulate and torment them, continuing to reiterate that he was justified in his behavior because the MHW had "come on to his girl." He also wanted the small female MHW to come in so that he could "talk to her" about his feelings of frustration.

The other nurse in the room reinforced that we were all in there to support him and he was welcome to speak with us.

But only a petite female MHW would do, according to the patient. He then asked to have his toe looked at and bandaged; a small laceration was present and I cleaned it off and put a Band-Aid on the wound. It seemed odd to me that he only had such a tiny wound to show for the damage that he had done to the heavy door.

I wondered if he would strike out and try to hurt me while I was helping him. But there was no time for ifs and buts, no time to reflect, no way to avoid what was, after all, the task I had to do. Many times, you have to just crack on and hope the patient will see that you are, after all, on their side, trying to help them in whatever way, doing whatever it was that they asked you to do.

Once again, we all turned our attention to the evening list of chores and activities on the unit. Not long after settling back into the routine, there was a flurry of activity over at the nurses' station. The patient in seclusion was banging on the window of the door of the locked room. He was demanding to go to the bathroom. It had been something like forty-five or fifty minutes since we had last offered it to him and we were due to go in and reassess him in about ten minutes. The charge nurse decided that we had to honor his request immediately.

I wondered what was going to happen. I was on guard, watchful, suspicious, and conscious of something afoot—but I knew not what. Not yet. But something was amiss, and the air felt different—the tension, the milieu, everything felt ominous. I felt "it" coming without even knowing what "it" was, because my intuition told me that the patient was planning something. It felt as if he was catching us off guard, taking conscious and deliberate advantage of our weakness in the moment, as though we were all vulnerable to some sort of attack in the seclusion room. I was not positive that we would be set up for success because we needed more staff for a show of support. We had called for other staff to come and help.

But would they even show up this time? Were they "too busy" on other things?

I called down to the campus police and asked that the officer who had come to our aid earlier, the one who had wielded the taser, should come up to our unit.

But this time, the dispatcher said it was a no-go; the officer was now off campus, transporting a patient back from the local hospital. So, now my patient was also coming back into the middle of this chaos. It all felt as though we were very vulnerable if we went into the room without all of our resources available, so I asked if we could put off going in until the officer was back on campus.

The charge nurse felt that we needed to meet the patient's needs immediately, since it was deemed that it would be an infringement on the patient's rights if he were made to wait a minute longer. I was officially overruled in my request to wait for the officer's return.

Staff went into the seclusion room to let the patient use the restroom. However, while we were accommodating the needs of the patient in seclusion, the other twenty-three patients on the unit were still engaged in their usual evening activities. An MHW was handing out evening snacks in the pantry located down the hall and on the other side of the seclusion room. Another MHW was doing the safety check rounds.

An MHW who had been injured by a patient the previous week was at the nurses' station, performing the light duty task of monitoring patients who require constant observation over the video feed. The only male nurse on our unit, the new graduate, and a couple of male MHW's went into the seclusion room to allow the patient to use the restroom. The charge nurse and I stayed out in the hallway, to keep the area clear in case things didn't go well in the seclusion room and a hasty retreat was required. I was worried that someone would get really hurt or killed while in the seclusion room if the patient decided to strike out. I felt he was simply spoiling for a fight and the whole unit felt very unsettled to me.

The enormity of the potential situation also gripped me; it felt as though we were delusional in thinking that we could possibly have the capability to deal with this sort of aggression and violence if it sparked. I remember thinking that the Crisis Prevention Institute (CPI) training we had all learned to use to defuse violent situations seemed far too ineffectual for the events of the evening, far too remote, far too theoretical, and more than a touch unrealistic.

Mostly, I just wished that the campus police officer would come back.

Patients continued walking around and were obliging with being redirected away from the area near the desk. Most times, patients who had been there for any length of time would instinctively know to move away from any area when directed by staff. This was very surreal because, with the door shut to the seclusion room, we were still a part of a very dangerous situation, but life was just plodding along on the unit with few disruptions.

One of the male patients started down the hallway from the cafeteria toward the male annex. He would need to walk by the seclusion room to get to the annex, so I asked him to, "Just wait a couple of minutes to come by the desk, please." Without any acknowledgement, he turned back toward the cafeteria, and out of the corner of my eye, I saw him spin around and pull his clenched fist back. I sensed that he was headed towards us with the intention to really hurt someone.

I remember thinking that this was crazy… that this volatility had come from nowhere, and that this patient had not demonstrated any sort of aggression to staff before. It showed how much we had to be on our toes, how quickly things could turn in a matter of seconds. In the change of shift report, we had been told that he was "just being his usual self" and still refusing to take prescribed medication. I now wondered if he wanted to hurt me because I'd asked him to stay back for a few minutes. His face was filled with hatred, contorted, and I thought, "I think that I might die because he looks like he is going to kill someone. If I die, I will never see my kids again."

The last thing that I remember was how I backed away, saying, "NO, NO, NO" and trying to step yet farther away… But I heard a loud cracking noise by my right ear, felt my feet come off the ground, and then… nothing.

I don't know how long I was sprawled, unconscious, on the floor.

In a state of semi-awakening at some point, and as if in a far-off horrific dream, I distantly heard a man yelling, "He's fucking trying to kill a nurse!" I wondered who was being killed and how I could help them. My eyes opened and suddenly I was hit with the realization that I couldn't see out of my right eye. I was all alone on the floor near the HVA. I thought I must be dead; well, if I were still alive, wouldn't somebody be near me or trying to help me? I slowly worked to move onto my hands and knees when a huge wave of nausea washed over me. While unpleasant, it was a little reassuring because I felt sure that dead people should not experience nausea. So, I concluded that I was still alive, still in the world, although right now, this world did not make any kind of sense.

My feet struggled to grip the slippery flooring; it seemed my shoes were off, and I was in disarray, my glasses and name badge gone, too. Without my name tag, I was essentially locked into the unit. I knew that I had to find my glasses if I had any hope of getting away, and all the while, the big and burning question was—*why aren't they helping me? Why is no one coming to my aid? Why have they abandoned me here like this?*

They, of course, meant my colleagues. They meant the people who, like me, had supposedly been trained to deal with adverse and violent incidents, such that they would come to their colleague's aid and know exactly what to do. Well, here was an adverse and violent workplace incident, and it felt as though there was no one to be seen. Not a soul.

I was alone on the floor, on all fours, with my racing heart, my panic, my pain, my enormous fear, my nausea and disorientation—and a tremendous sense of hopelessness washed over me. I didn't know what was coming next.

It was bewildering and confusing, but one thing shone through in its clarity: I was completely, utterly, on my own in this nightmare.

I was now also terrified that the staff couldn't control the perpetrator—the patient—if he got away, and I couldn't escape because I was struggling too much, with my head being so foggy and feeling so nauseated. I managed to get to the chart room where I sat and thought, "I really need to finish charting." Crazy nurse! The nursing supervisor appeared and asked me if I would like an ambulance to be called... what? You want me to figure this out?

So, of course, I told him not to bother; I didn't want to cause any attention to be drawn to me. I said this because I quite honestly didn't know what else to say. I had no clarity, and needed help, not questions.

He said that it would be good to be checked out at the hospital.

"...but my charting isn't done," I reminded him. "Besides, I don't think that I could drive." I think that this would have been a good time for a health professional to take charge and actually make the decisions regarding my care rather than asking the one who had been punched, kicked, and unconscious for much of the assault to figure out how to proceed. This was not care. This was putting more pressure onto the victim of the assault while they were in no fit state to make decisions with any kind of rational thinking.

In retrospect, I feel so angry that I could cry at how I was not cared for that night.

I ended up feeling abandoned, used, disposable, and somehow at fault for this whole mess. I told the supervisor that I didn't think that I could drive myself to the hospital and just needed some time to be in the restroom; a place where I thought that I could be safe behind a locked door. I could hear the patient yelling and was concerned that he would get free and come back after me. At no time did I ever feel like anyone actually cared for me, or even stayed with me, to reassure me that I would be safe. I can honestly say that I have never in my life felt so vulnerable or so alone.

The supervisor offered that campus police could take me over to the hospital.

We arrived at the cruiser and I saw a pile of papers on the front seat. I said, "Please tell me that you aren't going to make me sit in the back." He sighed and moved stuff and off we went to the ED. He pulled up in front and asked me if I could get into the building by myself. Of course, I said that I would. When I got to the hospital, the care there was casual at best. No one was too concerned about a nurse showing up bruised and battered. I was a horrible historian, for sure. The doctor asked if I thought that I needed a CAT scan. *What is the matter with people,* I wondered?

First, I have to figure out the transportation and now the diagnostic tools, too?

I asked the doctor what he would want if I were his mother. He was clear that he would want her to have a head CAT scan, of course.

I texted my daughter's boyfriend to ask him to tell my daughter that I was at the hospital and what had happened. I couldn't bear to break the news to her myself. She, in turn, contacted neighbors and asked that they check on me so that I wouldn't be alone. My neighbors arrived at the hospital and stayed while I heard the results of the CAT scan. I live alone so they were prepared to take care of my dogs and help me get my car home. One of the evening secretaries from the psychiatric facility arrived to drop off my work bag, forgotten when I'd left in the police car to go to the nearby community hospital. He was kind and offered that the staff on the unit were being well cared for by Assaulted Staff Assistance Program (ASAP) providers.

I said that it would be great if there was an ASAP provider to talk with me. I wonder if anyone at the facility even thought about offering that.

Just as an "aside" here, I need to explain how, through all of the night following the attack, I didn't even know what had occurred to me while I'd lain unconscious on the floor. The injuries I had sustained were certainly way more than from one single punch—the punch I recalled. It was only the next morning that I found out from campus police what had occurred while I was unconscious.

The patient had continued kicking me with his hard-soled shoes while I was out cold on the floor. At last, I could understand where my other injuries and bruises had originated. The entire back portion of my neck was swollen and bruised. My left knee was wildly swollen and sore. My right hand sported a bruise in the shape of a shoe print. The rest of my body had many sore spots and bruises in a variety of areas.

Bearing in mind all of this, doesn't it just seem even more surreal that the staff around me just post-incident were asking me what to do and what I considered the best course of action was? Why couldn't they see how desperately I needed to get seen in the ED, and just do it...

Anyway, I felt that nobody seemed that interested in looking at anything other than the head injury, even in the ED. Nothing else about me seemed important to the folks at the hospital. I was just a battered skull; the rest of me didn't matter.

So, here I was, on the receiving end of how it felt to be the one in the ED. And how it felt was miserable, lonely, and—to some degree—invisible.

I had spent the night in the hospital, waiting to see if the subarachnoid hemorrhage (SAH), bleeding between the covering of my brain and the skull, would expand and require emergency surgery. Yes, I had skull fractures, traumatic brain injury, SAH, and a huge concussion along with multiple other bumps and bruises, sprains, hematomas, and contusions. Yes, I was awake all night wondering how this was going to work… horrified and confused about the noise and lights all around me. I was nervous about the patient behind the curtain on the other side of the room. Then, it was humiliating that I was ordered to use a commode at the side of my bed with little privacy, and then that I had to ask for a way to wash my hands after urinating. That's just basic hygiene and patient care, isn't it?

I worried about my son and daughter being so far away and wondered who would help them through this mess.

Yes, I had been abandoned by my workplace… not one phone call to me or my kids by anyone in management. I was the one who called the supervisor to tell him that I wouldn't need a ride back to my car because I was being admitted. I still might need an emergency surgery if the bleeding expanded in my head. Yes, I was still really angry and not willing to accept excuses for any of this lousy and incredibly unprofessional treatment. In fact, it is against the law in many states to abandon a dog at the door of a shelter. This begs the question: why was it permitted to do this to a severely injured nurse in front of an emergency department?

When the sun finally came up, I asked what the plan was for me. Once again, there was no communication or any idea about some kind of timeframe for what was going to happen. My first visitor appeared... the hospital chaplain, who had been requested to see me by the nursing staff. Apparently, the day shift charge nurse on my unit at the psychiatric hospital had called to see how I was doing. My nurse offered that, "Physically, I think that she's going to be okay, but I'm not sure about emotionally." When the charge nurse at the psychiatric hospital asked if anyone had been in to see me to provide some emotional support, the nurse taking care of me seemed confused by the idea and offered that she wasn't really sure who would be available for that. While I was away at a follow-up CAT scan, the psychiatric hospital chaplain stopped by and left a plant on my bedside table.

The next person to show up was a nurse manager from the psychiatric hospital, with a brochure for the Assaulted Staff Assistance Program; it felt as though she was significantly out of her comfort zone. She stayed at my side and listened in when the campus police came to see me.

Her main concern seemed to be about calling the CEO of the hospital to tell him that "the governor didn't need to stop by after all" because she thought that I was going to be discharged and not sent to the operating room. Apparently, my assault was going to provide a "feel good" photo opportunity for a political statement...

Well, with my commode still at the bedside, that would have been a great photo shoot.

I sometimes wonder... if he had shown up, would the way that workplace violence was handled at that hospital have changed? Or would it just be another feather in a political cap?

As the police officers took my statement, I was finally told what had happened to me while I was unconscious... that the assault had continued until another patient disregarded directions from the staff and stepped in to stop the assailant from continuing to kick me while I lay unconscious on the floor. It was made abundantly clear by the officers that I was simply evidence of a crime committed. It would be up to the State to file charges against the patient.

So, where is that courageous and compassionate nurse so eloquently described in the medical school application personal statement? What does her future look like at this point? Fear, uncertainty, isolation, and shame are part and parcel of the physical and emotional injuries I suffered. There was little or no plan organized for healing. I was expected to simply muddle through and get back to work.

***

I hope it is reasonable to think that a healthcare worker will be provided a safe workplace in which to practice. Is it just me, or is that a healthy and vital provision for healthcare workers?
No healthcare provider should believe that being attacked while caring for patients or clients is ever acceptable, nor is it "part of the job." Acceptance is complicity; complicity is support of the status quo. This piece of the status quo is shameful. Unmitigated violence, and mediocre care for the victims of it, have no place whatsoever in a healing environment. I refuse to accept this treatment or be complicit in allowing any of my co-workers to be treated this way. I cannot support the current culture... and I will not be silenced.

Chapter 11:

What's the Plan?

One might think that my workplace would have had a protocol/ algorithm/plan of action for sorting through the maze of the aftermath of a violent assault on staff. I mistakenly *did* believe just that. In fact, not a second would have passed in which I'd even previously questioned if such a thing existed, because it was so obvious there'd be one. Wasn't it?

When going through orientation, I had learned all about trauma-informed care and how we, as healthcare professionals, needed to incorporate the theories in our practice.

So, of course, there would be someone calling and explaining the next steps to me, right? Trauma-informed care tenets would surely be applied to employees who had suffered a trauma in the workplace. There must be a plan in place to help me sort through all of this murkiness. I was a valued and loyal employee who took her responsibilities seriously. Mine was not the first episode of workplace violence in this institution, after all. The reality of the gravity of my situation started to settle in, and I realized that I was well and truly in a much different spot than I had hoped; I was repeatedly shown that I couldn't have been more wrong in my thinking about how I would be treated as a victim of a workplace assault. My faith had all been remarkably misguided and misplaced.

Statistics from 2018 show that 88.6% of the psychiatric nurses surveyed had been the target of verbal violence, and 56.1% had experienced physical violence in the past year. Horrifyingly, only 2.6% could lay claim to having no exposure to either physical or verbal violence.

Another survey, published in 2019, collected data from nurses working in a large forensic psychiatric institution. This survey demonstrated that support offered to the assault victim through the workplace—peers, management, and administration—provided a better sense of well-being and safety post-assault. In other words, healing in a supportive community can mitigate the damage caused by workplace violence.

Social support from friends and family can also be beneficial. Remarkably, 28% of the nurses surveyed post-assault in this study received no support either in the workplace or outside of it. Please let those two bits of information marinate for a bit. What I understand now is that my experience of isolation was not unique in the world of workplace violence.

After I was dropped off on the doorstep of the local hospital, before any assessment was made or care was given, the primary concern of the admitting clerk was to establish who would be paying the bill. The clerk quickly connected that I was a "Workers' Comp case" since I had been assaulted while on the job.

Years ago, I learned that the easiest way to tell if an egg has gone bad is to put it in a bowl of cold water. If it floats to the top, it is past its prime. It is still good to use if it sinks to the bottom.

Unknowingly, like a "rotten egg" that floated rather than sinking, I had arrived on the surface of the water. Now, I was no longer a useful item and was sent down the Workers' Compensation (WC) chute. In that one moment, my employer was relieved of any accountability or responsibility for what happened to me. They could not be sued for any wrongdoing associated with the assault, since they are relieved of any liability for employees receiving benefits on their Workers' Compensation plan.

Since I had been the victim of a witnessed assault, there was a silver lining for me and my family. Even though I went down into the morass of Workers' Compensation, at least I did continue receiving my pay and benefits from the workplace. Others, who work in institutions with different rules, may suffer severe financial constraints accompanied by finding themselves and their dependents suddenly without health insurance. Knowledge is power and, unknown to many, the Workers' Compensation program is a potent piece of protection that deals employers a winning hand and injured employees a losing one.

One of the many truisms, which I learned from growing up and living in the rural Northeast, is that life can be cruel and treacherous. While we love our wildlife, we also know that nature can be harsh. Not unlike the injured animal who finds itself culled to the edge of the herd, I was now tucked on the edge of no man's land. The unfortunate animal that finds itself in this unenviable position is vulnerable to predators and the harsh realities of nature. It soon became apparent that I was no different from the lame creature in the wild.

I had been assaulted during the evening shift on June 26, 2017. By lunchtime on June 27th, it was decided that the bleeding had stopped increasing in my head, my condition was stable, and I was finally free to go home. The PA who saw me handed me a note that said that I could return to work in two weeks and be assigned to "light duty" work. No lifting or physical contact with patients was allowed. Being a dutiful sort, I made sure that the paperwork was faxed off to my workplace before my discharge, and my neighbors were called for a ride since I wasn't allowed to drive. I was, once again, left alone on the curb to wait for my neighbors to arrive. A hundred bewildering thoughts still milling around in my brain.

There is an expectation that nurses demonstrate empathy.

While we may not have actually experienced what patients are enduring, we need to have the ability to look at the experience from their viewpoint. If I have ever not been kind and compassionate to a patient with a head injury involving traumatic brain injury, I sincerely apologize. Having a broken head is like trying to drive without a steering wheel and your foot on the gas pedal; you may still end up going places, but don't have any control over what direction you take.

For the first few weeks, I struggled.

A constant headache and accompanying nausea were my companions. Everything seemed insurmountable—and I do mean everything. Figuring out food was treacherous since my eyes were working independently from each other. The pantry was not well stocked and I didn't have a simple way to get food. Sitting in a moving car was courting disaster since I might need the driver to pull over in a jiffy if I had to throw up. Dogs were sometimes fed twice or waited too long to be fed at all, and my meals were missed completely. Some days, I thought I had eaten when I hadn't, or I looked for something to eat when I had just eaten it. I lost track of the days of the week and the times of day, merely stumbling from one moment to the other, and from one room to the next. I would get to a place and wonder why I had come there, or even how.

Some days, I sat on the floor in the corner of the kitchen, which seemed like a safe vantage point with the wall against my back on two sides, and I just waited to see what was going to happen next. From being a responsible, organized professional who cared for others, I had become, quite literally, a seemingly endless series of mishaps in the making.

The physical challenges were sufficient to cope with on their own, but these were still met in full force by psychological hurdles. The first night that I was at home, I realized that it wasn't safe to sleep when it was dark. What if the patient who attacked me was out? I live in a little town and we don't have a large police force... what if they didn't get there in time and he was able to further hurt or kill me? And, then, I started hearing things walking around outside of my house.

After a restless night, I realized that, like a drowning victim, I was going down for the second time and needed to get some assistance. Nurses and police have typically had good relationships with one another, rather symbiotic, in fact. I don't deny that this is not always the case, but our local cops have been kind and helpful whenever I have called. The police officer who arrived took one look at me... right side of face swollen and black, glasses askew, limping, and more than a little wild-eyed. He asked what he could do to help; he was the first person who asked that one simple question and then just waited for an answer. I told him the story of the patient assault and my fears of someone being around the house. He asked if I had someone who could stay with me for a bit.
Nope. Was I a gun owner? No. Did I have a dog? Two Shih Tzus;

not the most threatening guard dogs by anyone's standard! So, he offered that the police would always come if I needed them or, if I just needed to hear a human voice and talk about being afraid, they would listen. He told me that he had been in spots that were terrifying, too, and sometimes you just needed to have someone talk with you so that you didn't feel quite so alone in the mess. His final practical bit of wisdom was to make sure that the doors and windows remained locked and, something to think about in the future, might involve purchasing a gun. Okay, I thought, now I am getting somewhere with feeling a bit more stable in this situation; I finally have an ally, one who really knows where I'm at.

Somewhere in that fearsome fog, my soul ached for a comforting voice. I called a friend who has been much like a second mother to me for decades. As soon as she heard the story of the assault, she inquired if I thought that I had made a mistake by going to work at the psychiatric hospital.

I ruminated on that one. Perhaps she was right... it turned out, then, that it was my fault that this had happened. It was a mistake; my mistake. I was embarrassed and ashamed. I have since come to the conclusion that my error was to trust that the workplace would provide me with a safe place to care for vulnerable patients. My true error was in not asking the average annual assault rate per unit, how many work days had been lost due to assaults, how many injuries had required hospitalization, or what protocols were in place to help injured staff return to work and who was responsible for implementing those protocols.

Later that day, I finally received a phone call from work. A "human resource technician" was calling in reference to the paperwork faxed from the hospital regarding my return to work. She just had one question, "How do you possibly think that you can return to work with the physical restrictions listed?" I was gobsmacked. I didn't know the answer and she seemed quite impatient about my ignorance. I didn't know what criteria I had to meet to go back to work or how I was supposed to even get a follow-up medical appointment for care. The prescription to help with nausea was declined by Workers' Compensation pending approval of some unknown, powerful administrator; I didn't have so much as a number to call to get that sorted out. I couldn't ascertain how to manage simple, seemingly basic needs, never mind organizing the bigger picture. The technician's manner was curt and dismissive; the push to the edge of the herd was continuing, unbeknownst to me.

Mercifully, one of my co-workers stepped into the information void when she realized that I was lost. She offered to come over the following day and help me. Luckily, she had been down this road before and had a sense of what direction to take. Apparently, those who are hurt badly enough to require hospitalization for their injuries fall through the proverbial cracks regarding follow-up care. Finally, I had at least the very basic direction to go in so that I might stop sinking and tread water for a while. The upshot of the first follow-up appointment was that I would most likely not be going back to work in two weeks, as my other injuries needed to be addressed, and I would require occupational and physical therapy to regain full function.

The terror and anxiety continued to challenge me. I struggled to figure out who this person was, the one who had taken up living inside my battered body. It was clear that I had more than just physical issues going on and simply could not just ignore them. I was tasked by the WC case manager to "find someone" to talk to, but to make sure that they were willing to accept Workers'

Compensation insurance. I could write a separate book on the challenges of finding someone willing to take on the mess that I was rapidly becoming as a client. Plus, as the case manager offered with a giggle, didn't I know that this was probably the worst time of year to get hurt?

We were heading into the biggest vacation period of the year. Should have planned better, I guess. The ensuing isolation, combined with not being cleared to drive, provided me with the perfect Petri dish to start seriously going down for the third time; this round might just actually make me drown.

Another glimmer of hope beckoned me about two weeks after the assault. I received a phone call from my nurse manager. Perhaps he had some wisdom or support to offer, but no, he was calling to let me know that a JCAHO Sentinel Event meeting had been scheduled. I was welcome to come or not, but I should be prepared to be held accountable for what had happened.

I have since learned that establishing the "root cause" of an event may be easily translated to "assign blame, discipline, wrap it up, and go home."

On Saturday, not long after the meeting, the day dawned bright and beautiful. I was without purpose or plan for the day; totally without purpose, as I was still not healed physically, and felt exhausted by the demons chasing around in my head. It seemed that in spite of my good intentions and efforts, what had happened was somehow my fault. I was a disappointment and a failure. Daily, it seemed, I received shaming messages to that effect. And I was always alone. So alone. No plan, no understanding of how I had become the "rotten egg" being sent down the proverbial chute to the garbage can. Nothing I did was working, and it didn't seem possible that I could ever be good or worthy enough to be part of the world again. It was beyond exhausting.

If I had to go back to the same place where I was assaulted, it could happen again and I might end up dead. It seemed ill advised to try to deliver safe and competent care in an institution that had literally and figuratively abandoned me. How could I be part of a team when I could no longer trust the other players? I really didn't want to die on the filthy floor of a psychiatric hospital, but if I didn't go back there, what value did I have in the world? Any place was dangerous... it could happen again anywhere. Being a nurse was a big part of who I was, (and of who I still am) but how do I take compassionate care of the people who I am terrified might kill me?

My nurse manager had offered that when I returned to work, it was an expectation that I would provide care for my assailant... after all, "that's just what we do." And then I realized that I still did have some power; I had the choice of deciding how and where I could die. I could stop this madness and simply get off the treadmill. The world was already going on quite nicely in my absence and it would, most likely, not miss even a fraction of a beat if I was gone. I didn't want to die; I just couldn't stand living like this anymore.

Tricky business trying to talk to folks on a glorious summer Saturday. I just needed to hear a human voice, someone—anyone—who would pick up a call from me. I was at my lowest, and saw no point anymore. As I write this, I could cry just thinking about the ache I experienced that day. My son was the first person who answered his phone, and when I heard his voice, I started crying. The tough old mother must have sounded alarmingly broken—

perhaps even embarrassingly needy. He called his sister and, in the spirit of doing something from over a thousand miles away, they made the decision to call the police because they were afraid that I might harm myself. They were right to be concerned. My plan was well organized and low impact for whoever the poor soul was that found me; if anyone found me. I have, over the years, heard so many trite judgmental comments around dying by suicide; I would ask that you not waste your time moralizing about or judging me for my plan. While I didn't want to die, I was just finished trying to make sense of living. I didn't have a lot of options.

I now can honestly say that this current version of life was so foreign and exhausting that I couldn't stand being ground down for another day. I had, officially, gone under water for the third time and was ready to let the waves take me.

This time, a different police officer arrived at the door with his hand on his gun. First question he asked was from a textbook. "Do you have any weapons?" And then he actually looked at me and inquired why I was so sad. How could I even begin to answer? It was shameful what had happened and I was ashamed of it happening to me. I had nothing left. I was terrified that this police officer might make the decision to put me in handcuffs and take me away for a psychiatric evaluation. Fortunately, that did not happen. Hope may come from odd places and this was the day that I saw a glimmer of it. The officer pulled me onto a life raft. He told me that it wasn't my fault and that the whole mental health system was broken. He had transported patients in restraints to my hospital. He couldn't understand how people who were so dangerous that they had to be moved by armed police officers could be accommodated in a place where the staff members weren't protected. He told me that it was okay to be sad and angry. He asked me if I had food in the house, and said that he would be back when he was next on duty to check on me and see if I needed anything. He gave me his card and told me that he understood if I just needed to talk. He would never judge me because he knew what it was like to be scared.

That Saturday, my life was saved. Not by a manager or co-worker, but by a police officer who did not even know me. But he was one who cared. Simply that.

Remember in the beginning of this chapter when I observed that healing in a supportive workplace culture provides a more positive outcome for victims of on-the-job violence? I made an interesting discovery when I challenged the culture of isolation forced on me by my workplace. I found out much later that the hospital where my assault occurred has an "unwritten rule" of staff not being allowed to contact the injured worker.

We heal in community, not in isolation.

Time passed and I started to make progress in recovering from the physical injuries. Care was cobbled together in odd ways, for sure, but I survived. One step forward happened on some days, and it was three steps back on others. I lived in a state of almost constant panic. Nightmares were terrifying to the point that I was afraid to sleep some nights, and men raising their voices caused me to have chest pain. Loud noises or people running toward me made me want to hide.

One of the hot topics regarding healthcare workplace violence is how to deal with the aggressors. Many suggest that the perpetrators of a physically violent act need to be put through the legal system and punished. While this may seem logical, we need to remember that the victim of the assault will be re-traumatized at every step of the legal process. Also, there are no guarantees of the assailant actually being found "fit" to be punished for their actions. This was my experience. The investigating officers made it clear that I was, quite simply, evidence in a case to be presented to the Grand Jury. It was up to this group of people to hand down an indictment, indicating that the Grand Jury had found enough evidence to deem it necessary to send the case to trial.

I had no voice in whether this process could be stopped. What I did have was a demand for all of my health records for the defendant and his attorney, multiple calls about the rights of the alleged criminal versus my rights as a victim, and delayed notification when the patient was moved to a less secure facility and, finally, free. He was deemed unrestored, but not a threat.

This loosely translates to game over for the legal process and that he was free to move about in the community. The legal system, while the prosecutor and victim/witness advocate were kind and diligent, is not equipped to do much. Each layer of the process only served to repeatedly pick the scabs of the healing wounds.

My life assumed a routine of waiting to see what would happen next... just showing up each day and getting through to the end of it was a solid goal. Dust settled, and a supportive team of care providers emerged. There was no room for any long-term plans or dreams... I didn't really know who I was anymore, but it was obvious that I was not the person who clocked in at the beginning of the shift on June 26, 2017. It seemed that I was simply existing until I died.

The Universe does have a way of kicking us soundly in the

britches. In 2019, my son was in his last year of medical school in New Orleans. A wedding was being planned and it was scheduled to happen a month before graduation. Being part of a large, emotionally charged event with so many moving pieces is probably challenging for almost anyone. It took a grand effort on my part, which I fear, often fell short of the expectations of others. In retrospect, I can now accept that being around that many strangers in social situations was beyond me.

Hindsight is a powerful tool when seasoned with self-compassion and acceptance.

The week of his wedding, another important event also happened near New Orleans in Baton Rouge, Louisiana. I learned soon after returning home, that a nurse had died from injuries very similar to the ones inflicted on me. These injuries had also occurred during a patient assault. Just when I had settled in, once again, the Universe swift kicked me in the derriere...

Lynne Truxillo, the nurse who died that day in Baton Rouge, no longer had her voice; but I still had mine.

Chapter 12:

What I Don't Know Can Hurt Me

I look back and realize that my career offered so many opportunities to have been a better advocate for myself. Why would I look at laws, resources, or even admit that the unthinkable act of workplace violence would happen to me? Besides, I had far too many other balls to keep in the air with my juggling act of work, home, family, and school. In hindsight, replacing those assumptions with a very small piece of knowledge could have given me a tremendous amount of power. Being prepared by, as the old expression so aptly says, 'knowing the lay of the land' is useful. Understanding your rights and where to find help could, in fact, save your life.

My assumptions of a safe workplace, being valued and cared for by my employer, and the world at large being invested in the safety of healthcare workers were all repeatedly proven false on this rough post-assault ride. I will let a little light in, now, on what I know now that I wish I had known then. We often learn from our own challenges, but I am going to share mine so that you get the benefit of experiencing vicariously where I have found some of the larger bumps while navigating this windy road.

The first assumption that needs to be discarded is the notion that healthcare workplace violence will never impact you. Closely connected to this is the notion that 'people' will care about the survivors of workplace violence. Simply stated, others may have their own agenda, and healthcare workplace violence may just not be anywhere on it. There are many educable moments ahead of you; first, I encourage you to collect data and assess the available resources for dealing with the aftermath of violence. This knowledge may never be needed, and I hope that it isn't. The reality is that you will be well served by having thought it through before disaster hits. I am not planning on having a house fire, but I have always made sure the house insurance bill is paid on time. Knowing your rights and what laws are in place before the information is needed allows for the opportunity to be at the ready to advocate for yourself and others.

Thus far, I have resisted the temptation to write a checklist. It has been painful, but I have managed to avoid it. Out of respect to any healthcare workers and their loved ones, I am presenting this topic in checklist format; it is the format that works when there is a list of important issues to address, I know. Also, it makes me happy when I can check a completed task off the list!

Write in this book, make notes, have discussions with your family and peers. Use the checklist as a framework for asking questions to find answers before you need the information. Read that last sentence again. Do it before you need it; that's the crux. That's what will save you.

While I keep my fingers crossed that you will always be safe in your workplace, I know that many of you have found or will find yourselves driving over the bumps of healing post-workplace assault.

Important disclaimer here:

This chapter, like this book, is NOT meant to take the place of professional advice and treatment. I support and encourage you to seek the advice of trusted medical, mental health, and legal professionals as needed.

Please remember that this list is based on the classic, "If I only knew then what I know now." Everyone is faced with their own unique challenges and while some may be similar to mine, others may be entirely different.

Checklist

For many people, multiple benefits for employees and their families are tied to the employer and the workplace. What happens if you are injured in an episode of workplace violence and unable to work? Will you maintain your health and dental insurance coverage? Will your family's coverage continue if you are unable to work? ☐

If you are unable to return to work, at what point will your employment be terminated? ☐

What will your income be while on Workers' Compensation? If you work two jobs, will it cover the income from both? If you work overtime, will that add into the calculations? ☐

Do you know where to access data about the incidence rate of violence at your workplace? Severity of injuries? Average number of lost work days? I asked these questions at the interview for the position where I was injured. In retrospect, I remember that the nuts and bolts of that question were seamlessly avoided by the interviewers. In reality, absolutely NO data was being collected by the employer on this issue. It was not voluntarily or mandated to be collected by the employer or any governmental oversight. Documentation of the violent event was written to focus only on injuries sustained and not the violent cause of them. This format allowed the trail, which would also have allowed the statistical retrieval of violent incidents—providing both qualitative and quantitative data—to immediately grow cold. ☐

How do you document an episode of workplace violence? Where does this documentation go? Who reviews it? What feedback will you receive regarding its review? ☐

Is your facility mandated to report violent incidents to a government agency (such as OSHA)? ☐

What is the protocol when someone in your workplace sustains significant injuries due to a physical assault while on duty? Who advocates for the injured healthcare worker if they are unable to speak for themselves? Who is responsible for calling the emergency contact for the injured worker? ☐

Confidentiality: what is the law, policy, and procedure for maintaining confidentiality when an employee is injured by workplace violence? This may vary widely depending upon the area in which you work. I found that I had little or no privacy regarding the assault or my injuries. In fact, I was shocked to see my name and list of injuries published in the statewide newspaper. ☐

Is your employer proactive or reactive to episodes of violence? Is there a place for frontline workers to share insights, suggestions, and concerns? ☐

What is the workplace protocol for handling the emotional impact of an act of violence? What is their immediate response for the victim of the assault? The worker's family? The witnesses? The patients/clients? ☐

What is the background and training of the emotional support resources available in the workplace? How are these resources utilized? How are they notified of an event? How are the interventions they provide evaluated for efficacy? What are their confidentiality policies? ☐

What do you know about the Workers' Compensation Insurance in your state? Are you allowed to choose your healthcare providers if you are assaulted in the workplace? What are their confidentiality policies? ☐

What is the purpose of retaining a lawyer after sustaining an injury from an assault? ☐

What is the best timeframe for securing the services of a lawyer? ☐

What criteria are important for you when considering legal representation after an injury? Lawyers, like other professions, vary widely in skill sets. The person who helped to close on your house sale or the attorney who crafted your will may be the only interactions that you have had with the legal profession; personal injury and Workers' Compensation is a very different legal arena. Ensure you have a specialist in mind already—before any incident occurs. Don't just take the word of a friend or relative that "they know someone who's good." Trust your intuition about who would work in your best interest. Seek true experts and ask them ahead if they will help you in the event of an injury at work. ☐

What are your rights regarding access to care (medical and mental health) under your state's Workers' Compensation? ☐

What mental health resources are available in your community? Do you have access to a 24-hour crisis hotline? ☐

Does your workplace culture allow for communication between employees after an assault? Are there policies, written or unwritten, prohibiting your colleagues from contacting you after an assault? ☐

If you live alone and don't have family nearby, what is your support system if you are assaulted and need practical and emotional help? ☐

This list may be missing items pertinent to where you live and practice. Feel free to expand your line of inquiry. While it is horrible to think about being the victim of workplace violence, knowing your rights and resources is important. After all, we buy fire insurance before there's a fire, right?

Chapter 13:

Stillness

I live with dogs, that's right, plural. If I want to get the attention of my canine companions, I usually just have to mention the word "treat." Those of you who also travel the world with a four-footed buddy or two have probably seen this one-word wonder in action, too. Usually, when I offer said item, a frenzy of excitement and chaos ensues. The search for the object of their desire takes precedence over all other activities. When their human, blessed with opposing digits, finally opens the jar and distributes the coveted goodies, the whole atmosphere changes. There is a sense of fulfillment and satisfaction. Stillness settles in the household and the wolf pack enjoys a feeling of contentment. In my experience, the visual of my pups frantically racing around bears a great deal of similarity to the thoughts and feelings churning in my broken noggin after the assault. This distress and anxiety may be the yin to the yang of stillness. Let's look at the restorative effect that stillness may offer.

I have no doubt that there are many people on this planet who, for whatever reason, find themselves desperately searching for the sense of peace that my dogs demonstrate after receiving the blessing of a biscuit. At times, we find ourselves overwhelmed by frantically looking for something to which we can't even assign a name. Most often, this frenzy is happening in our heads while our outward appearances are of calmness and serenity.

Years ago, I remember commenting to a colleague that I had a great deal of admiration for how he managed himself in an emergency situation in the operating room. He responded that while he was glad that he seemed as cool as a cucumber, his internal reality was markedly different. In his mind, he felt as though he was wildly waving his arms around like a windmill in a windstorm and shrieking, "Nothing I'm trying is working! We are so doomed!" over and over.

Outward appearances may not be telling the internal truth. In fact, they're probably not telling it. Embracing self-awareness allows us to connect with and manage the noise booming inside of ourselves.

I found stillness remarkably elusive after I was discharged from the hospital. My house was eerily silent, but I did not experience stillness. As a matter of fact, strange as this may sound, the more silent my environment was, the less still my mind seemed to be; the proverbial inverse ratio. Nobody at the hospital explained how important brain rest was for healing the head injury I had sustained in the assault. Perhaps, because I am a nurse, I was just supposed to just know to put brain rest into my own plan of care. Without that guidance, however, I searched desperately around the clock for any distraction to take me away from the reality of my life. Literally, around the clock.

Not much worked, though; my physical head was a little too broken and hurt far too much to be distracted. I could not find the switch to turn the speed and volume down, of those insane hamsters racing madly around on the exercise wheel inside my mind. I was not unlike the dog madly looking for a treat... except, perhaps even more frustrating, I was desperately trying to navigate the unknowns dropped in my lap. My purpose circled around, looking for the answers to the queries of "what next" or "what am I supposed to be doing?" Coupled with the confusion about the future, I was the beneficiary of a great deal of what I like to refer to as "analysis by way of ignorance and hindsight." I would have welcomed kindness and support, but was ashamed and humiliated by what had happened. It was all my fault, right? Many of the questions asked by those who seemingly meant well reinforced the notion that this whole mess was somehow my fault.

"Do you think that he would have stopped if you had held your ground?"

"Do you think that you made a mistake by going to work there?"

The lens through which I was looking became increasingly tinted by what people were saying and doing. Now, I was stuck in a hugely uncomfortable spot in which there was a great deal of critical replaying of the event coupled with a distinct lack of vision for the future. Personally, I found that as I continued to sail off into uncharted waters where everything previously established as the norm was gone, it was beyond tricky to get any sense of stillness in my mind. Not unlike my colleague with the image of his flailing arms, I found myself feeling as though I was slowly steaming through every hour with my hands covering my head, repeating endlessly, "What am I supposed to do now?"

Combine this with the grandfather of all headaches and you can well imagine that stillness was more than a little elusive!

I just need to stop for a minute and make an important distinction. Stillness, while it embraces quiet and an absence of movement, gives one the opportunity to hit the reset button to gain focus and control. I liken stillness to letting the dust settle. Stillness is most certainly not the same as silence. In movies, we have all heard the expression, "maintaining radio silence." What does that mean? It refers to a complete cessation of communication. Silence is tricky at best, devastating at worst, for someone struggling with finding direction to navigate out of a situation similar to mine. Silence easily becomes part and parcel of their overwhelming isolation. Dreadful things can happen in isolation. Silence, left to its own devices, can simply grow and spread. In the absence of communication, issues aren't addressed and are simply allowed to continue perpetuating negative thoughts and behaviors.

Silence, post violence, has the potential to cause harm; not just to the most recent victim of violence, but to all who have or will experience it. When a coworker, friend, or family member is attempting to regain equilibrium from the impact of workplace violence, supporting them in the process of stilling their minds and bodies can be very helpful all around. Similar to opening the door to welcome in a herd of stampeding wild elephants, maintaining silence only allows the malignant remnant that results from that violent experience to grow and thrive.

I have learned that the ability to achieve a sense of stillness is a balm for healing and managing the emotional and spiritual wounds. These invisible, yet very present, injuries, fester and amplify without acknowledgement and care. Stillness provides the atmosphere to not only regain clarity and focus, but also just take a breath. Think about looking at a clear glass jar of water with a covering of sand on the bottom. Give that jar a solid shake and try to look through it... not very clear at all, is it? Now, stop agitating the jar and let it settle; it's a whole different view, isn't it?

So, my friends, this is the fun part. How do we achieve stillness? Sadly, no protocol or algorithm is handed out to those of us who could use it... basically, all of us! My pantry was sadly lacking ingredients for this part of the recipe, so much of what I used in the early days were very basic substitutes for a cohesive practice.

Here we are at the deep end, about to dive in.

People around you may be curious about what exactly happened when you were assaulted, and you will find that the details can be a fascinating topic of discussion for someone who has not experienced violence. People you barely know will crave to know the many ins and outs of every small detail, no matter how distressing it may be to you to be asked and to be expected to relate these intricacies.

The details are what matter to onlookers, just as folk drive more slowly to stare at a car accident.

Hot on the heels of the titillating details come questions that may feel judgmental, critical, or just plain silly. I learned that not unlike other news stories, there were opinions that folks felt driven to share with me and those around me. I felt like a container of French fries spilled on the beach, with seagulls ferociously picking away at what remained of me after the assault. I'm sure that when my story was worn out, those seagulls simply moved on down the beach to the next juicy tidbit. If interactions with folks don't serve your healing well and only muddy the waters, feel free to not expend your energy on engaging in providing the play-by-play of a traumatic experience. It has nothing to do with them, and everything to do with you.

I learned that I am not in charge of rallying the neighborhood troops around the issue of workplace violence from a victim's perspective. It's my story to tell and I get to decide when and whether I will tell it. I learned to let go of interactions that didn't serve my healing, and eventually, like the cream on raw milk, the people who respect your need for stillness and support your healing will rise to the surface.

I found that tucking in on the couch with my little Shih Tzu, Henry, was a positive way to pursue stillness and decrease the buzzing of the wild thinking going on in my noggin.

When Henry snuggled up against my chest, I could put a hand over his heart and through simply resting it on the rhythm of his heartbeat, I was able to focus solely on a living rhythm, taking a much-needed break—in stillness, for a change. Sometimes, I would simply sit with Henry on my lap and rub a thumb over the pads and fur of his paw repeatedly. Mindfulness, a powerful tool to help refocus and stay in the present, can be powerfully facilitated with the presence of an ally like Henry. Keeping my mind solidly in the here and now gave me a safe distraction from the chaos running circles in my mind. Plus, I felt less alone and far more comforted with my four-legged companion near me. This may sound basic, but in both of these instances, a simple activity provided temporary stilling and peace.

I mentioned taking a breath earlier in this chapter, something of which I have acquired a much greater appreciation since it was almost permanently taken away from me during the assault. Night was not a friend for me in the beginning, and honestly, sometimes it still isn't. Sleep was elusive, at best, or absent at worst. My daughter and I have joked in the past about being woken up in the middle of the night by malicious gremlins pulling at our toes. We have lightheartedly attempted to personalize the grinding thoughts that won't allow our minds to stop, so that we can rest in the hope that it makes them more manageable, I guess.

Being totally consumed with worry and racing thoughts is not only exhausting, but also definitely impedes healing. The gremlins can be positively crippling after workplace violence… thoughts about what could have happened, what did actually happen, what being dead might be like, and will I ever feel safe again, what happens now, what are people thinking, what is the plan…?

So many questions, so few answers.

Just take a breath, and another, and another… focus only on your breath. No fancy breathing required; just do what comes naturally. Inhale and exhale. Don't allow that myriad of bleak questions in; only focus on your breath and just keep breathing. Crazy as this sounds, I learned to play a mental game of the classic "whack-a-mole" to banish gremlins. Each time another troublesome thought would pop up, I smacked it down by just breathing. Give it a try, yourself. It may take some effort at first, but once mastered, it can be a simple and available technique to open the way for stillness at any hour of the day or night.

In the past, while a patient was waiting to go to sleep in the operating room, I worked hard to help them stay focused and calm. There is always a lot of activity before anesthesia is induced; I picture it as being similar to what must go on in the cockpit of a commercial jetliner as the pilots get the clearance from the tower to taxi to the runway. We all know what is about to happen and that it is meant to keep patients safe, but it is a time in which the patient is perched on the precipice of losing control of the situation and putting their complete trust in people they may only have met a few minutes ago. Stress and anxiety become like cooking a poached egg; perfect one minute, with just the right texture to be enjoyable... and a hard-boiled, inedible icky bit the next.

Engaging and remaining connected when the feelings of anxiety begin to overwhelm is a subtle art. Helping patients to be grounded in that space is key, not unlike when we are overwhelmed by those crazy squirrels running about madly in our brains.

I have learned that one of the strategies I've used when partnering with patients to help them through this stressful time works well for me, too. Here it is, so feel free to give it a whirl.

Close your eyes. Take a couple of slow, deep breaths. Take a little longer to exhale than you did to inhale; really, really let go of the air in your lungs. Picture, in your mind's eye, a place that you love a great deal, a location where you feel happy, safe, and at peace. I have had patients tell me that they took themselves to their favorite chair where they could watch the birds at the birdfeeder, and others have spoken about going to the top of a mountain recently hiked. It's all about you and your place. After you get this place solidly in your vision, expand on it. Use all of your senses. How does it feel on your skin? What does it smell like? What do you hear? Work to actually put yourself in that place. Relax, just stay there for a few minutes. Hold onto that overall sensation that spending time in this place gives you. Take a couple of breaths, allowing yourself to luxuriate in the sense of contentment that spending time in this sacred location allows you, and when you are ready—still holding onto that feeling in your gut—come on back to the world. I discovered that taking a break and spending time away from the chaos of the moment was a little like giving my soul a tiny respite. Sort of a holiday for your psyche if you will.

Focusing and remaining present to the situation at hand are life skills, which many healthcare workers already possess. These same skills can help with furthering that restorative sense of calm, too. I would be remiss if I didn't mention that physical activity is also a big player in settling the mad rabbits that sometimes join the racing squirrels in our minds.

Any movement counts in my estimation.

No marathon training or experience is required. Just move. One caveat attached to this: looking up and engaging in what is around you is the key to success in having this work to still the mad rodents in your brain. Take the earbuds out, put your phone away, and just pay attention to the world encircling you. Focus on what you are seeing and hearing. I used to park in a lot which required a ten-minute walk to and from the building where I worked. I did this not because I didn't enjoy the thrill of parking close to the door for a mad dash in to start the day, but so that I would have a few minutes to walk back out to my car at the end of a long shift.

Sure, I was tired and had taken more than enough steps in during my shift, but that tiny bit of walking before beginning the long commute home gave me a space to shake out the detritus of the day and transition to being on my own time.

The practice of meditation has never been in my wheelhouse, and after the assault, I found that opening the space up for guided meditations sometimes resulted in getting in touch with thoughts and feelings, which only dropped me right back into the horror of the assault.

Honestly, I have a difficult time settling down to doing nothing. For years, I have always had my knitting with me so that I have a productive task in which to engage while I listen to shows, podcasts, live speakers etc., and my mind does wander if I don't have that repetitive activity. And, wandering may actually mean that I totally miss whatever is being presented because I am entirely wound up in what is going on in my brain. Late in life, I have learned that just sitting with my knitting can be quite meditative if I allow my mind to settle and have a rest.

If I am caught up in a hornets' nest of unconstructive thinking, I practice my version of meditation. Feel free to try it. This is what my "practice" involves:

- Move away from all the physical stuff attached to the hornets' nest
- Settle in where I am comfortable and grounded
- Take my knitting into my hands
- Take a deep breath in and out
- Visualize myself emptying all of the thoughts from my brain, as if emptying a trash basket into a dumpster
- Simply focus on the knitting, without any thoughts allowed

You can try your version and it does not have to involve any repetitive handicrafts if those don't appeal to you—or, if you find that they just add to your stress!

If you feel that you are in a place to seek the opportunity to engage in a more structured meditation experience, take a look on

the Internet. One of the places where I found some great guided meditations is on Dr. Kristin Neff's website:
https://self-compassion.org/category/exercises/#guided-meditations

Dr. Neff is one of the world's leading experts on self-compassion. She has put the science behind what was previously thought of as a very soft concept. Practicing self-compassion helps to open the door to begin healing in earnest. When we gain comfort and ease with being compassionate with ourselves, it allows us to improve our emotional health and be far more compassionate with the rest of the struggling world.

Yoga and related practices provide excellent channels for settling into stillness. There are so, so many sorts of yoga... truly something for everybody! While some may enjoy the more athletic aspects of yoga, I have found that it is a helpful practice to support connecting my mind and body with the goal of being grounded in both. This connection between my mind and body helps me to feel safe in my body, bringing the fight-or-flight feelings down a notch.

I know, that sounds very "out there," doesn't it? In the beginning, it sounded downright daft to me, too. Of course, my mind is connected to my body. A mind is not like a set of dentures that can be removed and put in a dish. Honestly, such an odd idea. It really would be great if we could detach our minds and stick them in sterilizing fluid overnight for a fresh start the next day—but alas, it's not to be. The racing thoughts, which take up much of our lives, the antithesis of stillness, get in the way of the connection between mind and body. Focusing on the physical sensation of restorative yoga enabled me to slow down and remove the jersey barrier between my mind and body, to allow mindful presence in the moment.

I could just settle and be peacefully still. Whew!

There is a little yoga studio near me. Every month, around the time of the full moon, they offer a class known as "restorative yoga." There, the teachers focus on guiding the class into poses held for longish periods, accomplished through utilizing props and adaptations to accommodate each participant's physical needs. Holding the pose for a longer time coupled with being in a comfortable space allows me to hone in on what I am feeling in my body.

My brain has permission to simply stop working quite so hard and is given the chance to re-boot. I find amazing stillness and a deep sense of peace when I participate in this class, as it allows me the support to settle and mindfully embrace the moment. I feel a little control come back into my life, possessing a tool that helps me to harness my response to stress. Squirrels, rabbits, and chipmunks can take a break.

Going to a physical class may not work for everyone, I get it. Life also does get in the way of committing to a specific time and place. I wondered if there might be some sort of opportunity that would be more accessible; perhaps some sort of online offering to fit in around shifts at work and family obligations. I also wondered if there was any group focusing on providing yoga classes for survivors of violence. Seems like a lot, right?

Hope springs eternal and, with a bit of good fortune, it paid off in dividends. Synchronicity leaned in and led me to a helpful place called Exhale to Inhale, a trauma-informed yoga practice based in Brooklyn, NY. Exhale to Inhale is committed to providing trauma-informed yoga classes for survivors of domestic violence. The majority of their offerings take place in facilities such as crisis centers or shelters.

In short, trauma-informed yoga instruction helps victims of violence to gain strength and heal by feeling safe in their bodies. While the primary mission of this organization is focused on survivors of domestic violence, Exhale to Inhale has expanded and begun offering regular online trauma informed classes for the general public during the COVID-19 pandemic.

Knowing what we need and where to find help to get it is often daunting. When life has dished out trauma and violence, opening the door to find stillness may feel like an insurmountable chore. Really, isn't it easier to just let the busyness of our brains and lives continue to run amuck? Isn't this so especially after a particularly challenging event? We have a tendency to just step over it all and keep ourselves busy, right? Well, I disagree with the "busyness" plan. Walking that bumpy road taught me that giving myself the space and permission to build a relationship with being still was the foundation that allowed me to begin healing with self-compassion, purpose, and clarity.

Bullet Journal #9

Most of us would agree that the whole concept of stillness centers around the absence of distractions and busyness. But what happens when we quiet our thoughts, hush the noise, and stop the commotion? We have a chance to re-charge and settle. This brief pause grants the opportunity to literally take a breath and be calm, so that we can move forward with clarity and purpose.

If this feels comfortable and safe for you... Please sit in your favorite chair, place your feet solidly on the ground, close your eyes, and just focus on paying complete attention to your breath... as you inhale and exhale. No need to practice any special sort of breathing – just breathe. Let your mind empty of all thoughts and emotions. (Picture yourself dumping a load of dirty laundry into the washing machine and closing the cover); just focus on your breathing.

Grant yourself the gift of doing this for five minutes.

What did you learn from giving yourself the gift of stillness?

-
-
-

Think about the last time you were with someone who was struggling to be still; what did you try to help them gain stillness?

-

-

-

Look back on your life and reflect on the actions of three living creatures (people or animals) who have helped you settle into stillness when you may have been challenged by a life event. Using color and shape, draw something that you feel represents each of these beings.

-

-

-

What feelings come up when you look at what you have just drawn?

-

-

-

What helps you to be still?

-

-

-

What are barriers to your stillness?

-
-
-

What is the first step that you might take to overcome one of your barriers to stillness? Write a sentence describing this step and what it would do to open the door to stillness for you.

Chapter 14:

'No Time for all that Nonsense'

When I was in nursing school, ever so many years ago, we learned about the principle of "secondary intention healing." The term doesn't give much away, but it is an important concept in wound care. This term describes the process that occurs to heal a wound that is extensive and involves the loss of viable tissue in and around it. Typically, the edges cannot be sewn together. Primary intention healing occurs as a clean, well-approximated surgical wound knits together without complications. Secondary intention healing is a more challenging effort than primary intention healing. The slow and deliberate filling in of a pressure sore is an example of secondary intention wound healing. Secondary intention healing requires extensive repair time, the potential for scarring is greater, and the risk of infection is higher. A key characteristic of secondary intention healing is that the healing has to start on the inside of the wound.

There are few among us who have not either experienced ourselves, or vicariously through others, the trauma of a nasty cut or abrasion speckled with obvious dirt. There may also be jagged edges, which provide the foundation for unique scars to form, serving as reminders of the event.

Life dishes out traumas and experiences which require care in order to heal. While the wound may not be apparent, it is still there. Unseen scars will remain. These injuries may not heal completely or without complications if we don't offer up some tender loving care. Remember, secondary intention healing occurs from the inside out. Thus, it is important to clean out the dirt and debris, care for the wound, monitor for infection, and be patient while waiting for healing to take place. Self-care is not so terribly different from supporting a spiritual/emotional secondary healing process when you think about the purpose it serves. It allows the opportunity to heal from the inside out with the possibility of minimizing further injury.

Self-care has almost become a cult buzzword. If you search online for it, you will get somewhere in the neighborhood of 3,540,000,000 results in 0.56 seconds. I know, because I did. Popular topic, obviously, but one with which many of us struggle. Fair warning: I am going to address this topic from a very personal viewpoint… no more numbers or references to be found in the rest of this "op-ed" chapter. I also need to make the disclaimer that the biggest part of self-care is allowing yourself space to learn what care it is that you need to give yourself; my journey will hopefully give you permission to reflect and shift your thinking.

For many, the idea of self-care brings visions of fluffy spa bathrobes, well-pedicured toenails, twinkly tuneless "mindful" music, and a face full of something that looks like uncooked bread dough with cucumber slices over the eyes. No judgment if that resonates with you and meets your needs. I say kudos for figuring out what it is that your body, soul, and mind require in order to recharge and, once again, greet life fully. I have arrived at a realization about self-care; it isn't what you do, it's *what it does for you*. I am going to be so brazen as to offer that we might want to modify our use of words and change up the notion of "self-care" to "self-nourishment."

A bit more history is in order first.

The word "nursing" finds its roots in the Latin word "nutrire." This word literally meant to nourish. (Perhaps we could all take a moment to give Sr. Catherine, my high-school Latin teacher, a small round of applause). I believe that there would be little disagreement that those who work in healthcare find themselves in positions of nourishing the folks they care for in many ways. We physically, emotionally, and spiritually provide them with sustenance in times of vulnerability and need, sometimes on what may be the worst day of their lives.

Somehow, many of us feel as though committing time to ourselves is a ridiculous idea; there's so much to do and no time in which to do it! We aggressively minimize our own needs and amplify the importance of tasks and chores. It almost becomes a competition to demonstrate who works the hardest and longest. I remember saying so many times, "Self-care? No time for all that nonsense!" as if it somehow made me a stronger person.

It's time to take a look at what we gain when we value nourishing ourselves and give ourselves permission to put energy into mindfully pursuing it.

Think about this scenario for a minute.

You receive a call from your best friend in the world (BFW). She or he has had a nightmare of a day at work; thanks to the calamitous goings-on, her or his life will be changed forever. This is the icing on the cake of a grueling month and multiple personal, emotionally charged acrobatic feats. Your BFW passed empty on the gas gauge about two counties ago and is now on the last fumes in the tank. Some may decide that this is an opportune time to expand on ideas about how "God doesn't send us challenges until we are ready for them." Or the proverbial, "Time to make some lemonade out of those lemons!" Or, my personal all-time favorite, "Put on your big girl panties."

It is always tempting to offer solutions that would, seemingly, fix or at least minimize any of the emotional distress being suffered. Watching your BFW stuck in a dark, smelly place full of raw emotion and uncertainty is most unpleasant. Perhaps suggesting a diversion would work well, since nothing feels better than making observations about the activities the BFW could do to gain some redirection, helping her to cast off the angst of all her emotions, right?

But will a shopping trip on Saturday really disperse the ominous cloud of spiritual, physical, and emotional exhaustion caused by the cataclysmic events of life at that moment? I would offer that a healthy dose of soul-filling nourishment might be a more positive agenda. When we are literally void of any resources left after navigating the stormy waters of the world around us, it is more than past time to refill our own tanks. When overwhelmed, it is difficult to know what to do to fix the problems. I find that this is usually a good point to take a moment and shift my thinking toward a manageable goal. I think that there's an old expression about the first step being the hardest; true words, indeed. That elusive step, when life seems to be overwhelming on all fronts, may be quite simple.

Let's pretend for a minute that what your BFW needs at that moment is for *their* BFW to simply stand by with cups of coffee in front of the both of you. Just be present and sit in the crap together. That's what feels right for her.

No pep talks, no post-game quarter backing, no judging or shaming; ax the platitudes, no minimizing of the emotions; just sit in that messy spot and indulge in coffee. I am not going to try to fool anybody into thinking that sitting in this pile of emotional sewage is pleasant. I am willing to bet that there will be very few exclamations of "EUREKA!" that come out of this muck; I am quite certain that those moments usually only happen on thirty-minute primetime TV shows.

Yet this messy, gooey, emotional puddle is sacred, according to author, facilitator, and life coach Heather Plett. She refers to it as "liminal space."

Liminal space is an anthropological term used to describe a transitional time, a passage if you will. When we spoke, Heather used the example of the young boy who undergoes a tribal tradition that provides his passage into manhood.

Think about the twelve-year-old going out to spend the week on a mountain by himself. That time and what he experiences on the mountain is the liminal space. He will not be the same person that he was before he sat in the thorns with the wildlife for that period. He will have made a transition to being different, also acknowledged as such by the group to which he belongs. That time on the mountain has meaning. Back to your BFW; that cluster of life-challenging events has left the BFW in a puddle of slimy bits known as liminal space. When you give your BFW the time and support to wade around in the goop and embrace those raw emotions, it allows for progression to the other side of the swamp. Does your BFW come out of the slippery bayou the same as they went in? The answer is quite probably no, but they will at least be on dry ground once again.

Some of the liminal spaces that have dotted the landscape in my nursing career have been tough. Life has also not always been simple and smooth and the mix of life challenges often blurs. Here, I mean to address healing from violence in the workplace as my primary goal; I encourage you to utilize any of what is discussed here to help you and others heal from any of the bumps and bruises that occur outside of the workplace, too.

It is good to remember, healthcare workers spend time with patients, families, and co-workers. It is not up to me to establish the impact of events in a person's life. It is also not up to any of us to judge what a person's response should be to the catalyst that preceded heading into the swampy liminal space.

Glancing back at some of what I have experienced in my own life, I see a rich patchwork of so many beautiful, messy, and devastating events. My mother used to say, "How would we know what soft feels like if everything was made of velvet?" I look back and see many spots constructed of scratchy material that bear no resemblance to lovely, plush velvet. Marriage, divorce, birth of children, loss of cherished pets, the natural progression to "empty nester," and the deaths of my parents immediately come to mind. Professionally, I have watched the birth of stillborn babies, seen children die on the operating table, and patients struggle with life-threatening and life-changing illnesses and injuries. I have also worked in hospitals where lateral violence was embedded in the culture. I've survived a violent workplace assault, to name a few.

Have I always allowed myself to spend time in the swamp? No. There have been many occasions when I have stepped over, pushed through, "soldiered on" and devalued the depth of the feelings that I was experiencing. After all, so many tasks needed to be done; who has time for all of that emoting? True confession time. I have learned, oftentimes the hard way, that not allowing myself the opportunity to "make space" as Heather Plett refers to it, didn't make the impact of the experiences simply go away. Rather, the swamp just rotted and moldered in some hidden place deep inside of me.

At this point, it is helpful to take a small detour and address some of the elephants in the room; judgment and self-judgment. That voice of harsh self-judgment, which may echo in our heads, sets up a cascade of all the correct elements to promote self-starvation rather than nourishment. After all, if we allow ourselves to acknowledge that we are suffering, it's easy enough to call it a self-pity party, right? And we all know that self-pity is for narcissistic whiners. Oh, my, look at how well I just did my element of judgment/self-judgment right there! Just like a jet revving its engines on the runway before take-off, self-judgment fires up our internal engines, allowing us to send similar shock waves of judgment out into the world.

Think about the surface of a calm patch of water; now think about how the appearance changes when you drop a small rock into that perfect surface. Self-judgment could be compared to the rock with all of the ripples it sends to others around you. If we don't allow ourselves the space to be vulnerable, why would we encourage those around us to embrace that luxury? So much simpler to devalue their feelings and move on to passing judgment.

I have learned that certain words and phrases provide clues regarding the direction that I am about to take. Words can indicate that I have moved past thoughtful introspection and into the arena of soul-crushing self-judgment. For example, the word "should" has become a red flare sailing through the sky. The use of the word 'should' often signals the beginning of the death march to judge myself; this path then sending me through a door that I would be wise to not open. If I honestly evaluated the merits and personal cost of the activity that I *should* participate in, I would wisely run away from it as if my hair was ablaze! Use of the word *should* stirs up fertile ground in which to plant uncompromising feelings of failure and shame.

I have also learned to take a breath and stop when I hear myself start a sentence, "I'm so..."

Most usually, I have learned that the words that follow are self-derogatory in a hateful sort of way. I have found that the following phrase allows the brewing of the perfect storm to support this shipwrecked thinking because it provides a "buy one, get one free" opportunity: "I'm so... I should have..."

Here's a fun fill-in-the-blank, right? Please, let me go first with an example. *I'm so stupid; I should have seen that coming.*

Ouch. It's an easy leap to expand the judgment we are heaping on ourselves to others around us. For example, how many times have we heard ourselves or others say, "Medical and nursing students are such pains in the a*s, always in my way! They think they're so smart, they should know what they're doing."

I dare say that we have all been in a new position at some point in our lives. No, we didn't know what we were doing. That was the whole point of trying to learn more; that was why we were students and why we were in training. We have all been ignorant about some sort of cultural twist, which probably caused the seasoned folks to look at us as if we were cretins. We may also have judged ourselves harshly for not picking up on the subtle nuances that would have helped us fit into that novel environment seamlessly. We expected we would be perfect and, sadly, we often judge others according to our expectations of ourselves.

A big piece of self-nourishment requires cutting the umbilical cord to self-judgment. Just stop expecting perfection in yourself and shut that voice down. Spending time saying hateful things to ourselves is not growth promoting; it's cruel. If we can chase that big old elephant out of the room, it leaves a much larger area to fill with self-nourishing. I have learned that being mindful of my amazing ability to judge myself and working diligently to curb the habit has been challenging. Part of what nourishes my soul is the benefit of letting go of unhealthy self-judgment and the resulting effect that that elimination has on my view of the world. Curiosity and compassion have been allowed to take root in the absence of toxic self-judgment and assumptions. I have noticed that the ripples caused by halting my expenditure of energy on judging others has morphed into a more positive use of that energy. I have learned that the door has opened to something nourishing for my soul: kindness.

Kindness could be defined as being caring toward others as demonstrated by generosity and helpfulness. I have heard people equate kindness with weakness. Perhaps, at one time, I might have agreed with this assessment. In the recent past, I learned that contrary to that rather mean-spirited notion, kindness is most certainly sharing one's strength with someone who is in need of it at that point in time.

When we stop that harsh voice of self-judgment and judgment of everyone else, we are in a place of healthy strength, which allows the door open to sharing kindness. Being kind lets in a breath of fresh air.

Should we expect to receive a bouquet and public acknowledgment for being kind? Maybe just a high-five? Where does the self-nourishing show up in this crazy kindness talk? As much as I love definitions of words, I probably love stories even more. I thank you for bearing with me for yet one more historical narrative.

In 2013, my father reached the venerable age of ninety. While his body was worn down, his mind was still nimble. I decided to throw him a birthday bash in the form of an open house at his Masonic Lodge. He likened it to being able to attend the lunch after his own funeral without having to die first. I still miss his perspective. I ran an ad with a photo of Dad in the local newspaper to spread the word about the upcoming "do" (that's what he called it). Not surprisingly, on Dad's big day, lots of folks stopped by to offer their good wishes, many unhealthy finger foods involving mayonnaise were eaten, and a good time was had by all.

Let's back up a bit and get some perspective on the life and times of the man being celebrated. Dad never moved away from the area where he had grown up. His years in the U.S. Army during WWII were the longest that he was ever away. He worked hard at his job in a wood-turning factory, attended church regularly, helped others quietly, paid his bills on time, and minded his own business. He was honest to a fault, and never one to mince words even if tender feelings were subsequently hurt. I do not think that he would have been considered by others, or by himself, to be a mover and shaker in the world. He was definitely not cuddly and cute. My father was the stereotypical New Englander... taciturn, gruff, non-effusive. He was a curmudgeon, through and through. The interesting part about that birthday gathering, though, was what one of the guests said to me.

A middle-aged man wandered into the crowded basement dining hall and scouted around as if searching for something valuable. I didn't recognize him, but was interested in learning more about why he was there. Before I could make my way to speak with this guest, I saw him shake Dad's hand, chat for a minute, and then head back up the stairs to leave. Intercepting him, I introduced myself and proceeded to inquire how he knew my father. The smile on his face was priceless. Apparently, many years ago, when this man was fresh out of high school, he had landed a job at the factory where Dad worked. He was a "wet behind the ears kid"–his description, not mine. The photo in the paper jogged his memories of how my father had treated him during his early time at the mill. Dad, by this man's account, was respectful, encouraged a good work ethic, and supported him when things were frustrating in a new place. In other words, Dad had shown this youngster kindness.

So much kindness, in fact, that this fellow felt the need, so many decades later, to take time out of a beautiful spring day show up at a party for the express purpose of thanking my father. Dad couldn't even place the man among all of the others that he had worked with over the years. People do tend to come and go, but Dad's legacy of kindness apparently went on forever. Dad smiled each time the topic of the "unexpected guest" came up in the conversation; it was nourishment for his soul, with dessert included, I think.

Now, here is the challenge. Just think about becoming your very own BFW.

Allow yourself to sit in that liminal space. Feel all the feels without judgment or criticism. Simply treat yourself to what you might do for a good friend, and be kind. When you are ready, make your way out to dry land. Acknowledge that you very well may have a shift in your perspective and allow yourself to be okay with that. In other words, allow the liminal space to be nourishing.

Self-nourishment happens when we set boundaries. We all hear about the importance of setting these things, but what does that concept of a boundary truly mean to you? What does it look like to set a boundary in your life? How does it feel when someone crosses that boundary? Even more strategically, how well do you respect your own boundaries? Have you found yourself making a plan to self-nourish, only to find that it falls apart because you sabotage yourself into thinking that this piece of your life may only happen when everything else is completed?

Establishing and respecting boundaries provides a grand start to opening the gates of self-nourishment. Several years ago, while working twelve-hour shifts with a long commute, I spent my days off helping my elderly parents. I was pleased to be in a spot where we could make certain that they had rides to appointments, lunches out, and errands done. On one of our many trips out to do what they considered necessities, I realized that I had arrived at the point of mind-numbing, saliva-drooling exhaustion. I thought that I was the only human capable of sorting everything out for my folks. The day had started briskly at 9 a.m., and, as we headed home at about 3 p.m., my mother offered that it must be lovely to have a day off during the week. A day off? What day off?

I had not had even a moment to myself!

I didn't begrudge my parents the help that they needed, but I also realized that I had set absolutely no limits or boundaries on what I was willing or able to do. My "day off" had been devoted to everyone else but me, and by the time I had got Mom and Dad safely home with all of their shopping put away, it was immediately time for me to head to my own house to tackle everything that was required so that I could keep my own home and hearth operating smoothly.

I had mistakenly thought that by being endlessly available and rarely factoring in any time for myself, I was a better daughter, mother, and nurse. I mean, who doesn't love to hear a co-worker talk about the monstrous list of drudgery that they accomplished on their "day off?" It is the stuff heroes and martyrs are made of, I thought. Actually, setting a boundary around taking time for my own self-nourishment would not only have been better for my mental health, but I also do believe that it would have probably made me more patient and kinder... and far less tiresome to be around!

So, over the years, I have discovered a few key pieces that help me to nourish my parched soul. Take a look at the following list and see if anything resonates with you.

Sufficient self-nourishment can sometimes be accomplished in the space of only a few minutes, so it really is something we each have time to do. Scheduling it in may make all the difference in how your day unfolds, so please do give it a try.

So, here's my list for self-nourishment. What would be on your list?

- Bingeing on programs on Netflix. Doing this without self-judgment is great when I need a little time away from the world, to rest.

- Decluttering. Clutter really does make me crazy; it's that sense of discombobulation that shows up when every flat surface in the kitchen is covered in thingamajigs and unfinished business, which really causes me to have a ramped-up sense of anxiety and disorganization. I find that it is worth the few minutes that it takes to clear some space so that I can feel more settled and focus on the business at hand.

- Curtailing my *to-do* lists. I need to say that again. You see, I LOVE LISTS. It used to be that the longer the list, the better I liked it. Now, I make lists containing only the important things. My lists also address the big projects in stages so that they are carved into manageable portions.

- Being grateful. The COVID-19 pandemic has helped me to appreciate people I had previously taken for granted; UPS drivers, for example. When a delivery happens, take a minute to let the driver know that you are grateful for their diligence. Doing this sort of thing makes me feel as though I have shifted some of the negative in the world into a more positive direction.

- Being kind to someone for no other reason than to be kind. I may never know the impact of my kindness, but I am willing to bet breakfast that it will definitely have one.

- Drinking the second half of my morning cup of coffee on the porch, helping me to ground myself in the outside world and experience a sense of calm so that I can tackle the day ahead

- Having a really nice bar of soap or some delightful shampoo in my shower; it makes me feel as if I am spending a day at the cucumber slice spa.

- Silencing the ringer on my cell phone and turning the computer off; sometimes, I just need to not be available to the world, and I also won't feel guilty for it anymore.

My self-nourishing comes from small movements that don't cost much in either money or time. They do help me to keep my tank from going empty when meeting the needs of others.

Not long ago, I was chatting with my daughter, Rachel. She and her partner had recently moved three thousand miles for him to take an essential position in a hospital system. She was also in graduate school. Just a few days before our conversation, she had started a new job. The proverbial cherry on top of this glorious chaos of life was that this was all happening during the COVID-19 pandemic. During our call, I asked Rachel how her day had been, and she matter-of-factly offered that it had not been terribly productive. I responded with a little comforting motherly mumble. Then I heard Rachel say something, which, for me, hit the mark on what self-nourishment is all about:

"I decided to just let myself be tired today."

Her plan was to take the day to rest and recuperate while honoring her sleep schedule. No self-judgment about being lazy, or struggling to push through. She knew that this meant that the next day would require peak effort and focus on getting work done, but she also felt sure that she would have the energy and strength to accomplish everything on the list efficiently.

Give it a try, as I think that you may find it beneficial. Take a moment to look inside yourself and validate what you need in order to be nourished, and then give it a whirl. If you want, take a whole day and make a meal of it—relish it and enjoy it! There are no rules, except that this is your time, time in which you will care only (or at least predominantly) for yourself.

Few among us would endorse starving our bodies of important, regular nutrition, would we?

We understand that eating healthy food provides the necessary nutrients to give us energy to do work, plus it helps to make us resilient to stressors. We do not always think of it but the same holds true for nourishing the whole of us... spirit, mind, and emotions. I firmly believe that when we take time to mindfully self-nourish, we not only heal, but also become more resilient in the face of a challenging world. Secondary intention healing at its finest, without a doubt!

Chapter 15:

My Soul Aches

What is it that makes each of us uniquely ourselves? While I am not a theologian nor a philosopher, I do believe that there is something sacred within each of us that makes us who we are. In this chapter, for the sake of simplicity, I will call this something a soul. Please, just stick with me to the end of this chapter; I am hopeful that what I say may strike a chord of recognition within you.

A few years ago, I had the opportunity to attend a conference about plastic surgery. While your immediate thoughts may turn to topics such as wrinkle fillers and breast augmentation, this conference had a very different flavor. The majority of the speakers were there to share their experiences and techniques learned while on mission trips where reconstructive procedures were the mainstay. These doctors performed grueling, complicated operations for no financial gain at all.

During this conference, one of the surgeons brought up the topic of emotional or spiritual income. In a calm and reassuring manner, he told the learned attendees of this gathering how the trips to faraway places filled his soul. His passion was touching and it allowed me to open the door to my own soul. As a nurse, I have often received far more from patients than I have given. I have had the privilege of accompanying patients as they traveled hallowed paths in life. I have helped babies be born, families grieve unexpected deaths, aided those with traumatic injuries, advocated for those who had no voice, and tended to broken minds and bodies. In short, I have seen many people on the worst days of their lives. In being present, I have given a little of myself to each and every person for whom I have had the honor of caring. This caring comes at a price, of course, but it also brings rewards.

The depth of my gratitude is boundless, for the privilege I feel at being able to help a patient undergoing a life-altering event.

Sometimes, the very people for whom we step up to care will lash out at us. When that violence is physical or verbal, it hurts our souls. These patients, the ones toward whom we are running so that we can help them, can seem to reach out greedily and suck our souls dry; they may not even intend to, but still it happens anyway. I have yet to meet anyone working in healthcare who doesn't have memories that fill their soul. Many have had their souls viciously bruised and scarred, and as you know already from my story and others told in this book, the many incidents of physical violence may result in physical injury to the healthcare workers who were only trying to do their best for their patients.

These obvious physical injuries may demand attention and treatment. Breaks, lacerations, and bleeding are difficult to ignore, awkward to look away from and to pretend not to have seen. It is simple and convenient to isolate the battered bits, apply plaster and bandages, and send the victim back into the game. Well, the show must go on. Sadly, the unseen injuries are repeatedly overlooked; all the battered, bruised, and drowned souls get lost somewhere in the muddle.

My first visitor at the hospital on the morning after I was assaulted was the chaplain from the psychiatric hospital where I worked. We had had some dealings while I was on duty and I had always found this man humble and kind. It often felt as though he brought a handful of peaceful fairy dust to our unit, as his demeanor was calm, accepting, and open. I was surprised that he would be the first to arrive in my room since I didn't think that I was really a member of his "flock" in any religious sense. He also made no assumptions at all about what had happened to me; he was a giver not a taker, in every sense, sharing with me his boundless compassion, understanding, and empathy, and making himself available to be on hand and to simply listen. And not only was he able to listen, but he was also one of the few who really heard me.

There is a difference, and it is profound.

He was not there to take from me anything, and he did not request it either.

He did not show interest or inquire after the sordid details of the attack—not how it commenced, or how it unfolded, or how it was sustained and then, eventually, brought to an end. It appeared that—refreshingly—he did not need to know the ins and outs of my injuries or how much blood there had been, or which bones exactly were broken. None of that. He wanted to know about my soul, my feelings, my fears, my spirit, to reach out to all of these within me, and just to be useful in whatever way that meant for me.

I will always be grateful to him for purely being there when it mattered, letting me know that he was available to help me in any way that he could. Even more than that, he would continue to call and check on me in the following months, and I don't recall ever receiving a lecture or any well-meaning advice on how to pick up the pieces of my life. He was, quite simply, there.

A little later that same morning, I received a second visitor. This was the hospital chaplain—not from the psychiatric hospital, you see, but from the hospital where I was receiving my treatment.

This man had been summoned to go see me by the nursing staff.

In fact, the day charge nurse from my unit at the psychiatric hospital called to check in on me, too, since she had realized that while the physical head injury was being treated and would heal in time, the emotional bruises and scars left by the violence still sat happily unnoticed in my hospital room. This had not even been acknowledged by a single staff member during that very long night. I owe my colleague a debt of gratitude for advocating for me, and for being the one who stepped up to think about the things that were bigger and more impactful than just the physical injuries.

While my bodily injuries were impressive, the laceration of my spirit felt more like a suppurating, festering wound that nobody saw and no one wanted to think about. The hospital chaplain was quiet and unassuming, politely asking if he could sit with me for a bit.

When it seemed right, he did ask a question—unlike the first chaplain—but this was so ridiculously (and unexpectedly) gentle and elementary that it permitted the floodgates to open.

"Would you like to tell me what happened?"

He, too, did not put any pressure on the matter, and he did not have his own expectations or agenda around the subject; he simply wondered if I wanted to share my story, and if that would help me? This seemingly unimpressive query allowed me, in a confidential and non-judgmental space, to open up and tell the story from my perspective, without feeling my personal space or my psyche were being violated. He would accept whatever I felt able to share, pushing me no further.

I did talk, and freely, and the words came stumbling from my lips as if they were glad to be set free. It was difficult and it was painful, but the unburdening felt good and right.

I talked about all of the emotions that overwhelmed me. I spoke of my horror the night before when, regaining consciousness, I questioned if I was actually dead; it made no sense to me that I had been left lying all alone, and being dead was more rational.

I spoke freely of my anxiety about what would happen to my family if I couldn't work. Sadness overcame me when I realized that if I had been killed that day, I never would have been able to tell my kids that I loved them one last time. I had also spent the night afraid to sleep in a strange place with an unknown patient on the other side of the curtain. Fear, frustration, and a sense of helplessness bubbled out. I could finally just tell the narrative and acknowledge the horror of what had happened, and was no longer being questioned by campus police, or having photos taken on the lieutenant's phone for "evidence." I wasn't part of a discharge plan or anyone's checklist. It became clear that listening to my story was the only thing taking place in the room at that moment–no critiquing with the other members of the team, no assigning blame to me, and no retrospective review of my actions. Suddenly, I was in a position where I wasn't in charge of knowing the answers or the plan… I could just feel. I could just be me.

When I worked in the operating room, calling the hospital chaplains was considered a bit like the football "Hail Mary" play. Yes, indeed, I did that intentionally. When we started to run out of ideas in our roster of medical magic to turn a dire situation into a happy ending for the patient, it was time to call in the cavalry of damage control, the chaplains.

They would willingly drag themselves out of bed in the dead of night to slip into whatever hideous corner of hell in which we found ourselves roasting, and I believe that they always did it with kindness and grace. The chaplains spent many hours and drank gallons of bad hospital coffee while sitting with the desperate families in the surgical waiting area. At times, no words were spoken and no group prayers uttered... the chaplains just attended with their presence. Sometimes, people just needed not to be alone, and the chaplains grasped this perfectly.

For this book, some of the nurses interviewed spoke about a deep and abiding faith, which carried them through some of the dark moments in their lives. For many, the simple act of praying would help to gain strength and determination to return to frightening workplaces. One nurse described her pre-work routine of praying for the patients, staff, and safety of all as almost grounding her in preparation for the long shift ahead. She affirmed that she wasn't heading in alone.

At this point, I need to add in a bit of a disclaimer: I am not devoted to any particular brand of organized religion. I have no membership card in my wallet with admittance to a specific congregation. No chain around my neck identifies me as a member of a special group. I just try to get along with everyone and not be a jerk. It would be grand if others could do the same, but I do understand that it is a challenge on a daily basis. I really do understand. But I believe that we have that space within us that touches and is touched by others. Some might call it a soul or spirit. Like other parts of our beings, it is possible for this unseen portion of what makes us who we are to be neglected or injured. The plastic surgeons at that conference understood this; this was why they took time out of their busy lives to fuel their souls. The chaplains who visited me that day also understood the importance of mending the wounds that weren't necessarily visible on x-ray or CAT scan.

Focusing on healing can be an insurmountable challenge when the soul has been battered by workplace violence. Change is challenging. From where I sit, I have seen that humans crave "sameness." We cling tenaciously to the idea that we can maintain the previously known and comfortable. If we just try harder and push against the present reality, we can get back to "normal."

Violence, though, acts as a catalyst that can shift the victim's view of the world. Following a violent attack, the victim may find that nothing appears the same. Even the smallest of things is being viewed as if through fresh eyes. That which was once familiar, too, has become foreign and alien, and in some cases, quite scary.

Reclaiming the balance enjoyed before an assault may be impossible, yet it is still desperately sought. Victims walk a tightrope in this spiritual pandemonium, looking for a source of non-judgmental support after an episode of violence to accompany them on this journey.

I know that I did.

As I have explained, the information contained in this book is meant not only to acknowledge the devastation of violence in the healthcare workplace, but also to share resources for healing. I do love finding and sharing resources. My hope is that you will have options and open doors to help navigate your healing process. Take what you need, please.

Curiosity may have "killed the cat" as the old saying goes, but mine led me to a pearl that is well worth sharing with those of you sailing through the rocky waters of workplace violence. Looking back on my interactions with the hospital chaplains, I questioned what role facility chaplains might play in the bigger picture, and what this group of professionals brings to the table to assist healthcare workers. One thing I note, too, is that the hospital chaplains really do not care what faith you adhere to—if any—or what denomination you are; they just want to support you in your hour of need. They care for your soul in a manner of deep concern and warm empathy that perhaps only this role can successfully deliver, since it certainly doesn't come naturally to most people.

The Association of Professional Chaplains is a dynamic organization of members from a variety of religious affiliations. The first step in becoming a chaplain involves being ordained or endorsed in a faith group. In addition, specialized education in the chaplain role provides the members of this group the education and practical experience that enables them to deliver care in hospitals, long-term care institutions, hospices, rehabilitation centers, military, and correctional facilities.

This organization has more than 5,000 member chaplains and affiliates. These chaplains have accepted the job of attending the spiritual needs of all while respecting diversity, abilities, and beliefs. Tall order, right? Moreover, these 5,000-plus souls are doing this work in facilities often plagued by desperation, disaster, fear, and a feeling of all-pervading hopelessness.

I was moved to explore more about this mission. Most importantly, I learned that the role and training of chaplains is quite different from that of a minister in a parish. Rather than addressing the needs of a specific congregation sharing the same faith base, chaplains are available to provide support to everyone connected with an institution in any way, regardless of religious affiliation. To gain entry to this specialty, in addition to the religious education required to provide pastoral care by different denominations, certified chaplains must complete a specialized clinical pastoral training and residency program. Chaplains are special in the sense that they work very much in the "here and now" when something horrible may be happening. Their job is not to give direction, but to listen and provide support. Chaplains, although members of different religious denominations, do not bring their own viewpoints and biases to the situation. They simply attend in the moment, step into uncomfortable situations, and walk beside whoever is struggling.

During the COVID-19 pandemic, for example, many chaplains have found themselves supporting not only patients and families, but also staff across a wide range of hospital departments. I quickly realized that I needed to actually connect with someone who might give me a deeper understanding of the intricacies involved in hospital chaplaincy resources.

'We cannot heal what we don't acknowledge.'
Chaplain Joe Perez

Enter Chaplain Joe Perez.

Chaplain Perez, or Joe as he prefers to be called, is the current president of the Association of Professional Chaplains. He is also the spiritual leader for two hospital systems. That is quite a lot of spirit to be leading, I think—certainly more than enough for one man! I believe that Joe has seen a few wild and crazy situations in his decades as a chaplain. I found him to be a kind, compassionate, and engaging listener. Cold calls are stressful for me, yet when I called Joe, I immediately felt at ease while speaking with this stranger who was a couple of thousand miles away.

Joe stepped into describing the role of chaplain in concrete terms. Chaplains are trained to walk into situations where strong emotions and feelings are present. Painful feelings associated with the situation at hand need to be acknowledged for healing to begin to take place. He spoke of the chaplain's work in walking with people who are going through tremendous discomfort, without judgment or advice giving. Accompanying the suffering on this voyage helps to begin the healing through a process of acknowledging, affirming, and validating the pain caused by trauma. Chaplains bear witness to what is happening in sacred places of the lives of the people they serve; they sit in the alligator-infested swamp waters. I learned that there are no nameless "elephants in the room." Nothing is ignored in the here and now of a life changing/challenging situation. Chaplains have been trained to have the ability to address those scary elephants one by one, intimately and by name, and to sit comfortably with them, wherever they may show up.

We spoke of the epidemic of workplace violence and the impact that it has on healthcare workers. We spoke of the fear, sadness, anger, and isolation that often hang over a healthcare worker after experiencing workplace violence. I inquired what chaplains might offer to help staff who have been assaulted or have witnessed such violence? So much healing needs to be supported. After an episode of violence occurs, the path toward healing the bruises left on the victim's soul is best walked with a companion. This trail may have several tricky dips, turns, and hills; the terrain may be downright treacherous at times.

Joe observed that healing does not stop in one place; rather, it is a journey. He offered that to gain strength to carry the memory of a traumatic incident, it is key to be supported through the grief process around it. The trauma doesn't define all of the victim, but it does define a part of that person. Finding a sense of peace and an acceptance of that new defining part may feel insurmountable. The challenge of supporting any person walking this rollercoaster of a healing journey is the stuff that professional chaplains are well educated to do; they accomplish this through listening and accepting the traveler right where they are on that journey, without criticism or advice.

My various and sundry experiences with hospital chaplains added practical dimensions to the holistic healing process which Joe had so eloquently described. My favorite chaplain of all time was Fr. Mulcahy on the classic TV show, M*A*S*H*. Fr. Mulcahy seemed to be ever present and available to all, and he still said Mass for the faithful. I loved how he was simply present in all of the episodes of that timeless TV show – accepting, never judging. Those sassy doctors and nurses loved him, and Joe laughed when I shared my perspective on Fr. Mulcahy... he offered that he liked being in the same category as that classic TV hospital chaplain.

Nurses and doctors, on the other hand, are known for being reticent to ask for help. We are the ones who are supposed to always have an answer that will save the day. Like police officers and soldiers, we are meant to be in charge, not receiving assistance. Nothing is ever supposed to overwhelm or bother us, and every emotion has a drawer in which to be securely placed so that there is not a thing to distract us from our work. We are endlessly clever at capping our thoughts, feelings, and emotions, and veritable champions at compartmentalizing uncomfortable memories.

After all, we are warriors, right? We can simply plow on where others would falter.

Well, that's the myth, anyway.

When I was a new OR nurse, we had a patient roll into the operating room in the dead of night. This patient had been in a horrific car wreck. We struggled for what seemed like hours, but we just couldn't get any traction to turn the situation around. The extensive bleeding was impossible to stop, the vital signs were never stable, and the prognosis was grim. The entire room looked like a really bad crime scene. This was what is known in the business as a "non-survivable injury."

The adrenaline-driven actions of the staff were rapidly changing into a heavy sense of hopelessness. Folks who work in healthcare will recognize the feeling of time slowing down; everything starts to move in slow motion just ahead of admitting defeat.

In spite of our efforts on that night, we were failures; we couldn't save this life. At that hospital, it was an expectation that the nurses would call the priest if the patient was Catholic and the situation was heading in a catastrophic downward spiral. This priest would change into scrubs and come into the OR to give the patient the sacrament of the sick. I remember that, at times, when the faithful in distress had fallen behind in meeting their religious obligations, the priest would baptize, confirm, and give last rights as a kind of package in the OR. Having made every effort to save the patient that night, we decided that it was time to call in the priest.

Our own magic was finished; let the priest now deliver his.

After the priest had finished with the patient and left the room, he stopped by the window at the scrub sink. Looking up from our ineffective flail to save a life, the anesthesia resident and I realized that the priest was praying at the scrub sink. I believe that he may just have been blessing all of us. Sometimes, even the healers need blessings.

What is my take-away on healing a soul that has been wounded?

- Give yourself permission to face the feelings you are carrying about the difficult experience. Allow them to bubble to the surface, and be honest with yourself. Remember those sage words, "You cannot heal what you do not acknowledge."

- Access resources to accompany you on your healing journey.

- Recognize what your immediate needs are and honor them.

- Grant yourself time to gain equilibrium and the understanding that healing is a journey.

- Always remember that you are important and valuable; there is only ONE you! This is your trip to navigate at your own pace.

- You are deserving of the presence of someone who is willing to accompany you on the healing journey with kindness, respect, dignity, and non-judgmental support.

- Allow yourself to ask for and accept help; this ability is a sign of significant strength.

- Reject shame and blame by not imposing these on yourself and never accepting them from others.

The work necessary to climb out on the other side of grief is difficult, but it can be done.

Sameness may not be an option; all the parts will be different now, so you will need to find ways to embrace change and a fresh perspective. I believe that there is no returning to the way life was before violence intervened; that life is gone. I also believe that it is possible to heal and move forward to a new version of life. Your suffering has meaning.

Bullet Journal #10

If you were writing a recipe that could nourish your soul, what would it look like? Feel free to have some fun with filling in this very retro/vintage recipe card; don't forget to draw a picture of something that might represent the finished product.

Food for My Soul
Serves: ____
Ingredients:

-
-
-
-
-
-

Directions:

1.

2.

3.

4. (etc.)

Helpful Hints:

-
-
-
-
-
-

Chapter 16:

Finding Your Voice

We have all felt deeply about an issue at one point or another in our lives. I know that I have. Daily, I find that I read at least one social media post about an upsetting situation or unjust event. Predictably, the comment section takes off with a lively discussion around the various viewpoints spurred by the initial post. Passionate beliefs erupt, arguments are made, emojis are posted, comments may be liked, loved, or laughed at—but then what? Often, all that follows is the figurative chirping of crickets. Opinions have been expressed, but no actual progress was made regarding the initial concern.

I would offer that we are not remotely proficient at advocating for ourselves. Many of us limit our efforts to posting on social media. Those posts do little or nothing to influence or aid the negative situation; our ideas and opinions don't make it past the screen of those on our friend lists. I would venture to guess that the online dialogue might even serve to discourage and dishearten those reading it. The snappiest sarcastic comment can shut down all inclination toward taking positive action. Spouting negativity is easy; becoming a change agent often requires initiative, vulnerability, and a generous amount of elbow grease.

When I find myself falling prey to a defeatist attitude because of the prevailing "hopeless, hopeless, hopeless... we are so very, very doomed" theme, I think about where I live.

My house is located on a hill on a dirt road; I can reach it by either going up or down the road. The driveway leading to my house also requires going up an incline (which always seems much steeper in the winter, especially during inclement weather). When the hill that I live on has not been plowed during a snowstorm, accessing my driveway can be an exciting adventure. That's a bit of sarcasm, right there. It may seem counterintuitive, but I have learned that choosing to go up the road tends to guarantee success more often than opting to take the easy way down the hill to reach my driveway.

Going up the hill takes a concerted effort combined with a bit of finesse, but it gets me to my goal rather than sliding along and, perhaps, totally going off the rails in a different direction. I would argue that, not unlike my seasonal maneuvers, we might have to accept that success requires gathering focus, doing the work, and struggling up an oftentimes intimidating incline.

It is daunting to sort out what the best first step should be to shift frustration and anger toward healing and growth. When we allow ourselves to be caught up in the negative energy generated by a list of complaints fueling the idea that "someone" should do something to rectify a situation, it merely leeches our strength and enthusiasm. I offer that this abdication of power and responsibility could be replaced with the healing mantra of, 'I have the ability to do something', and 'I will do something about this.'

Essentially, it's about making a conscious decision to climb up the hill to access the final goal of positive change.

Without a doubt, the reality of expressing an opinion carries risk. Basing that opinion on fact, rather than emotion, will imbue it with credibility and assist in gaining traction when working on a call to action. I encourage you to allow yourself a little time to wade through personal feelings before stepping into any of the activities discussed in this chapter. I have learned to do this and it has served me well.

Here is a small laundry list of thoughts to mull over as you step into finding your voice:

- Not everyone will see your concerns as important. Some will dismiss them without any regard.

- Get in touch with your intuition and build a solid relationship with it.

- Some may not share the same degree of emotion that you have about the issue of concern. Some will seem completely switched off to it.

- Persistence and perseverance are key attributes to maintain when you find your voice.

- If one door closes, PUSH open a different one.

- Embrace the broader picture, also known by some as casting a wide net.

- Start and end with the facts.

- Learn to ask the "what" questions.

- Stick to the issue; not the emotion it provokes.
- You are a professional; do not discount your experience and education.
- Don't take it personally if your agenda is not considered important.
- A stakeholder is defined as a person with an interest or concern in something–someone with "skin in the game." If you are a stakeholder, validate and own that title.
- Privilege does exist in our world; if someone is not affected by an issue that concerns you, it may take more effort to enlighten and persuade that person of the real impact of the problem.
- Take an honest inventory of what tools and resources you have at hand. You may be surprised by how many you actually possess.
- Assess and nurture your strength and tenacity.
- You are a professional, first and foremost. Separate your profession from your job/employer.
- Practice stepping away from emotion and becoming almost dispassionate about the issue. "Just the facts, ma'am." Dealing only with facts will keep you on track.
- Focus on the issue; don't get your mind or argument tangled up in assigning blame to another person or agency.
- Being solution/goal-oriented helps with getting the message

across more positively than simply complaining. Suggest ideas for fixing the problem… even a small step.

- Use your voice to express gratitude and support.

- Remember that many of the helping professions are mandated by codes of professional ethics to work for social justice. Ah, there's a bit of power right there! Did you feel it?

- Think about how the issue affects you personally, in addition to how it impacts those you serve.

- Remember, very few wars are won after fighting only one battle.

- Elected officials work for you. Hold them accountable and give feedback.

I learned most of this through trial and error. The catalyst that spurred me into action arrived as a nasty surprise.

A couple of months after I was assaulted, I received a text from a co-worker. The message contained only a link to the statewide newspaper. Being naturally curious, I clicked on the link. There was an article at the top of the front page of the second section, which included my name and a list of my injuries. I was baffled that this could have happened. Health Insurance Portability and Accountability Act (HIPAA) protection for patients and employment confidentiality are gold standards for protecting privacy, yet all the information was sitting there in black and white for all to see.

I looked at the name in the byline of the article and opened the computer to search for his contact information. I could feel myself starting to morph into an angry lioness with a troublesome thorn in my paw. Unlike that delightful classic children's story, there was no little mouse standing by to help me. I felt violated by having my injuries broadcast far and wide without my knowledge or consent; I had become the spectacle everyone stood and looked at. Sure, in a way, this constituted "news" but I would wager that, to many readers, it was an entertaining read, nothing more.

My first call was to the Human Resources office at the hospital. The person who answered the phone seemed to struggle to understand my concern; she postulated that if I had been in a car accident, my name would have probably been in the newspaper. Trying to be logical, I observed that the other driver would have had his name published, too. This is different, though, she explained patiently. The assailant was a patient so he was protected by confidentiality and HIPAA, hence his own name could not be exposed for all to see. Oh, great. I see! So, I was fair game because I was the victim, not the perpetrator.

Well, what if I had been sexually assaulted? Would that also have been put in the newspaper?

Hmm. That had her stumped, albeit for a short pause only. With a chuckle, she offered that the good news was that this had not happened to me, since I had only been the victim of a physical attack, not a sexual assault. Therefore, it really wasn't an issue, was it? Technically, true. Should that have made me happy?

I wondered, what if the unthinkable act of sexual assault was to happen to a staff person at that facility next week? Would they discover themselves, along with the description of their assault, on the front page of the state newspaper? I felt a little bit of myself start the excruciating slippery slide down into some crazy unexplored rabbit hole where everything was foreign to my previous understanding of how the world was supposed to work. At what point did it therefore become acceptable to publish my details, and whose decision had that been?

Moving on, my next call was to the reporter named in the byline of the article. While kind and interested in my concern, he offered that he had merely found the information on the agenda of the Governor's Executive Council. This agenda was public information, he carefully explained, so anybody can access it. This allows the contents of the agenda to be fair game for the media to print. I was discovering that the crossover between politics and healthcare was indeed a murky, messy spot, and I had arrived in the middle of that confusing intersection.

At the end of our conversation, a door started to swing open and a light also began to illuminate what had appeared as a dark void; now, the reporter was offering that he would be interested in speaking with me about healthcare workplace violence. At that point, I realized that there was nothing left to lose by using my voice, and he could even be a megaphone for it.

I live in a small town located in a small state. We do have a limited claim to fame because we have the largest state legislature in the country (hats off to Mr. Dusseault, my high school U.S. history teacher, for imparting this information to me so long ago). We have what is considered by many to be a "volunteer" legislature because they receive a tiny financial compensation for their efforts.

My next call was to one of my local state representatives; I thought that since he represented me, he would care deeply about making changes to improve not only the lack of confidentiality, but also the issue of workplace violence. Think back on what I said earlier about mistakenly assuming that others would care about your agenda, simply because it matters to you; well, suffice to say that this was where I learned that bit of wisdom!

My state representative answered the call, but was out on the golf course, which—of course—was deeply important to him (and in fairness, I didn't much care about his game of golf any more than he was to care about healthcare workplace violence. But it wasn't my job to care about his golf...).

He didn't seem very interested in hearing any of my concerns, but I was irritatingly persistent. He pointed out that he was, after all, really just a volunteer and not paid anywhere near enough to tackle this sort of project. He would have to get back to me sometime in the future after he had connected with the "stakeholders" in the issue. Should I plan to be at this gathering? No, he said; only stakeholders would be included. Well, I wondered who could be more of a "stakeholder" in this situation than the person who had found herself sprawled and unconscious on the floor. From my perspective, that was solid "skin in the game." I offered to him that since this had happened to me, I felt that I, indeed, was a stakeholder. But no, they would not be at all interested in having staff nurses at the meeting. I do not think that it is a Yankee understatement to say that my first attempt at self-advocacy after finding my voice was a dismal flop.

Several shifts in my thinking could have made a difference in the productivity of these interactions. Perhaps I could have looked for an ally or advocate in my communications, or I could have done research on the representative's voting record. If I had done so, I might have chosen to reach out to a different state representative more aligned with promoting safe working conditions. I could also have taken several breaths before attempting to communicate with anyone about my concerns. I could have asked the "what" questions rather than charging in like an angry lioness with a sore paw. For instance, neutrally inquiring about the representative's definition of stakeholder would have provided me with clarification regarding the direction our relationship would take.

After a major regrouping to resolutely lick my wounds, I changed my approach and adopted a far more mindful manner. I knew that Massachusetts had recently passed legislation to prevent healthcare workplace violence in response to a violent attack on a nurse. (This is Elise's Law, known formally as 'An Act Requiring Healthcare Employers to Develop and Implement Programs to Prevent Workplace Violence'). I reached out to the Massachusetts Nurses' Association, a union representing a large number of nurses working in the Commonwealth of Massachusetts. This group had tenaciously labored for the passing of the violence prevention legislation. While not a member, I found the support and direction I had been lacking.

Clarity of purpose evolved, allowing me to gather facts about how to tackle my concerns. I was connected with a local ally who helped me map my path to speak out about not only the issue of workplace violence, but also the intrusion of my privacy. My ally helped me learn how to write an op-ed article that would meet the criteria to be printed in a newspaper:

Since that time, I have also testified before the NH House Labor Committee in support of legislation that would require public institutions in the state, not covered by OSHA, to collect data on the number of assaults occurring in those workplaces. At the time of my assault, there was absolutely no data available regarding the number of violent assaults; 'first report of injury' did not include the cause of the injuries. My testimony encouraged legislation requiring the Department of Labor to investigate those violent incidents. The legislation failed along partisan lines that year.

Without data, episodes of workplace violence remain only anecdotal and not easily validated. And of course, if a problem does not exist, then no solution is required, right? Lacking statistics, it was impossible to define the scope of workplace violence in public institutions in my state.

Every four years, New Hampshire has the distinction of holding the first presidential primary in the country. We see and hear from almost every single candidate running for POTUS. They have live meetings in small places, and their campaign workers can be found trudging door to door all over the state, seemingly also having offices in every nook and cranny. Most evenings, around suppertime, the good citizens of New Hampshire can look forward to receiving multiple phone calls from campaign workers, beseeching us to support their candidate. What a grand opportunity this political extravaganza provides! I realized that if I stepped up and showed up, I could potentially speak about my issue with the next President of the United States. If I supported legislation before Congress, I could ask the candidate's position on that legislation.

If it were to pass, would they then commit to signing it into law? I could share my concerns about the issue and its impact. Beautiful, right? Depending on which group in which locale happened to be sponsoring the meeting, tasty refreshments may even be offered.

Now, the majority of healthcare workers are employees of hospitals and other institutions, so we walk a fine line between speaking our truth and potentially incurring the wrath of our employers. This is, undeniably, a tough spot. Seeing my name and injuries in print, however, had solidified my understanding that I had nothing left to lose by speaking out. I was not even a statistic at that point; I was just disposable. I also realized that voicing concerns did not need to threaten either your income or employment; you are a professional with an ethical obligation to your patients and profession to advocate and educate. Therefore, I also would urge you to embrace your own professionalism and find your voice by simply using one of the tools that you probably utilize daily in the workplace: SBAR.

For the uninitiated, SBAR was adopted as a framework for both written and verbal communication in healthcare somewhere back in the 1990's. SBAR stands for Situation, Background, Assessment, and Recommendation. This formula helps us attain the goal of effectively handing off information to other healthcare providers to promote safer patient care. I have found that the SBAR framework provides clarity and focus in my thinking, even away from the patient bedside. Using this format when I speak up on the issue of healthcare workplace violence allows me to voice my concerns both professionally and succinctly. Hold onto this framework; I will discuss it and show an example of how it can be used.

Let's explore which options may be channels to raise awareness of important issues, hopefully before said issues turn catastrophic. As I mentioned, rants and emojis on Facebook and other social media may make us feel heard – but not necessarily by the people who can leverage our opinions, along with others like it, to forge the way for a positive change. I am sharing a list of options and ideas that can be utilized to facilitate your voice in the delivery of a message that could add sparks and, ultimately, start the fire of change:

1. Conduct online research to discover if others share your concern. Find a social media page/website/forum for your topic of concern (YTOC). There are multiple groups on social media platforms (open and closed) where significant interaction and education regarding current healthcare issues take place. This provides you with a starting point to gather more information and avoid the energy wasting exercise of reinventing the wheel. Networking is a real thing in our world and you may find a like-minded spirit who is geographically distant, but who will aid your efforts in ways that you can't begin to imagine. Of course, if no such groups exist, then you may be interested in starting one yourself.

2. Carry out a survey of professional literature on YTOC. If you have an online library affiliation through school or work, use it. If you have access to a physical library where you live, the librarian there can be one of your best allies in an information search. Honestly, my little local library is an undiscovered powerhouse of resources when I just ask the librarian for a little help. Google Scholar can also be accessed right from your smartphone. This is another fine option for finding peer-reviewed journal articles. I strongly suggest that you avail yourself of the "filters" which are options to help narrow the search criteria and are found on most of these websites. Stick to information published in peer-reviewed journals within the last five years.

3. Use your social media accounts to share YTOC among your friends and loved ones. SBAR it. Encourage action in the "recommendation" part of your post. Give the readers a clear channel for action. Ask them to post in the comment

section regarding their action. Reply by thanking them for the actions taken.

4. Write a letter to the editor of your local paper. Stick to the issue. If possible, reference a recent article in the paper, since that immediately shows you read it and that you are writing about something topical. Use the SBAR framework to craft your letter and incorporate that article as part of the "situation" paragraph.

5. Join a professional organization that addresses YTOC. There is strength in numbers.

6. Attend a professional conference related to YTOC. You can learn a lot from what others are doing to gain momentum in addressing the same issue you are tackling.

7. Don't assume that others won't be interested because they don't share your perspective or your educational background. Healthcare impacts everybody in some fashion. EVERYBODY!

8. Think outside the box. Videos have the possibility of illuminating and capturing the attention in ways that just using words does not. Photos or videos leave a stark imprint in our minds that calculated wording does not.

Take a look at the documentary video, "Code Black." A group of Emergency Medicine resident physicians made this documentary about training in the Emergency Medicine program at LA County Hospital. The visual images speak a million words. We all have an idea of what a "crowded waiting room" looks like; in the video, we look into the eyes of the rows and rows of people sitting for over twenty-four hours in that county hospital, waiting to be seen by a doctor. This form of communication translates your message on an undeniably visceral level, which, hopefully, transcends the partisan political morass.

9. Offer to speak with student groups. You have a unique viewpoint bred through experience. Share it with empathy and kindness. Think about opportunities for sharing a message that you think will be beneficial to all around. For instance, if you work in the operating room and find that you are impatient when accommodating students in that space, offer to help them learn the "house rules." Don't abandon what is important to you and the delivery of patient care by using the notion that "this isn't my job." You will find that attitude very, very disempowering. I know I did. Many medical schools offer their students the opportunity to join a variety of interest groups related to specialty areas such as surgery, anesthesia, or emergency medicine. Check in with the leadership of the interest group pertinent to your practice area and see if they would welcome having you speak about what makes your workspace unique, what the rules are, and answer their questions. Reaching out and providing this education before you are all bubbling along in the steaming soup pot of providing safe patient care will serve to decrease everyone's stress. Give yourself the pleasure of adjusting your attitude to one of justifiable professional pride, accountability, and responsibility. Allow yourself to step into some empathy for folks who are trying to play the game, but who didn't receive a copy of the rules that would help them be successful. Help them by voicing goals and expectations for students in the specialty area. Ask them what they hope to learn during their time in your clinical home. Be open, collegial, and honest. Maybe even bring a plate of cookies. Nothing says, 'Welcome to the neighborhood; I will help you settle in' quite like food.

10. Learn to tune into legislation relating to YTOC. Write to your U.S. Senator and U.S. Representative about it. Through the election process, they were hired to work for you. Adjust your thinking to become an interactive employer rather than a passive bystander. From where I sit, I have seen very few politicians who excel at mind reading. Our power of communication is an excellent tool to use to disseminate information about YTOC. Remember, it's the squeaky wheel that usually gets the grease. Speak up. Educate your friends and loved ones about YTOC. Offer them the instructions for emailing their elected officials. Send an email or call the office. Refrain from sending multiple emails… one well-crafted message will suffice. If they sponsor legislation that is important to you, or vote in favor of the legislation, then write another email to say thank you. When reaching out via email, I write a draft in a document and save it on my computer. This draft allows me the opportunity to revise, edit, and check grammar and spelling. When I have it tweaked to my satisfaction, I just copy and paste into an email. This step saves time and unnecessary regrets born of sending something off which has a glaring grammatical/spelling error or lacks clarity.

Here is a template that I find helpful to use for writing an email:

Thank you for ________________ (Something that they have done to support/promote something important to you.)

S: I am writing to you regarding ________________. Here is the situation. An example might be a rise in workplace violence locally. Perhaps you were a witness or victim of it. (Tell the story and the impact it had on you personally. Include how many years you have spent working on the frontline of healthcare and in what capacity.)

B: In a recent literature search, I found this statistic _______________ regarding the increasing rate at which this problem is occurring. (Background of the issue. Quote a pertinent statistic or professional article validating the scope and impact of the problem.)

A: I am concerned that if this issue continues, it will have a negative impact on both care providers and consumers by ______________. (Assessment of how this issue influences you and those you serve.)

R: This is your recommendation for addressing the issue. For example, if there is legislation regarding a solution, ask your legislator to support passage of the bill.

Thank them for the time and attention given to this important matter. Offer that you are happy to share more insight and information if they would like to contact you.

Sign the email with your full name and professional title.

11. Vote. Learn about the candidates running for election or re-election. Remember, they work for you. Evaluate and consider carefully which box to check in the ballot booth. After all, you are their supervisor. You are hiring them to accomplish work on your behalf.

So how does all of this hard work to find your voice and use it connect to the process of healing?

In the last chapter, Chaplain Joe Perez eloquently explained that after a trauma, healing came to incorporate acceptance of the part of you defined by the trauma. For me, that part was being the victim of a physical assault while on duty. The accompanying shame, blame, and neglect only served to continue the trauma. Healing began when I accepted that I could not go back to the person I had been before the assault, but I could allow my efforts after the violent episode to define that part of me as a survivor and not a victim. Finding my voice allowed me the opportunity to give space to workplace violence, acknowledge it, and speak out about its impact on healthcare. This is healing.

Chaos Theory is the branch of mathematics dealing with complex systems, the behavior of which is highly sensitive to slight changes in conditions; this means that small alterations can give rise to strikingly great consequences. In more practical terms, many of us have heard the analogy of a butterfly that flaps its wings on one side of the world can start a wind that results in a windstorm on the opposite side of the globe. Small changes make an impact.

Think about what could happen when you find your voice and use it to share your truth. Shake the dust off of your wings and move them up and down. No effort is too small or unimportant. Now, imagine if we all find our voices, the possibilities from the impact are limitless.

Bullet Journal #11

Have you experienced a situation that caught your attention, positively or negatively? The breadth or depth of impact can be enormous, or seemingly tiny. What matters is that it is something that you want to change and in which you feel empowered to send out a call to action.

What is a current challenge that is exceptionally important to you as a professional?

What makes this especially important to you?

What have you experienced regarding this issue? Does the issue impact others too? In what ways?

What have you learned about the bigger picture concerning your issue? Articles? Statistics? Peers?

-
-
-
-

Who are your U.S. Senators? What are their email addresses? What are their local office phone numbers?

Who is your U.S. Representative? What is their email address? What is their local office phone number? I am a proponent of calling, writing, or emailing elected officials and I encourage others to do the same, especially when it becomes imperative to raise our newfound voices in a call to action.

I did a little experiment; call it quality assurance, if you like.

My project involved calling the local office of one of the U.S. Senators who represents my state. Why? To check in and find out what happens when we utilize that mechanism for finding our voices. I understand that not all elected officials manage communication with constituents in exactly the same way but they are, nonetheless, all meant to be representing their constituents.

Here is a synopsis of my call:

Telephone ringing…

Office of U.S. Senator (OUSS): "Hello, you have reached the Senator's office. How may I help you today?"

Me: "Hi! I am interested in learning more about how to encourage and support others in using their voices to encourage change. I am especially keen to find out what happens when I contact the office of an elected official. Would it be okay to ask you a couple of questions about that?"

OUSS: "Of course, I will try my best to answer any questions or concerns you have."

Me: “Okay, so what’s the best way to reach out to my U.S. Senator?”

OUSS: “Calling, fax, email, or even snail mail works. Whatever means people use to reach out will be brought to the Senator’s attention.”

Me: “Is there any special format to use when calling or writing?”
OUSS: “No special format at all. It may be helpful to the caller to do a bit of research first, though. Just to check if there is legislation that has been written on the caller’s area of concern. If there is, asking the Senator to co-sponsor the bill and support its passage can give her solid information moving forward.”

Me: “Anything else that helps to get a message across?”

OUSS: “I think that mentioning the personal impact of an issue is good. That gives the letter or call more dimension.”

Me: “Okay, can I give this a trial run with a real issue that is incredibly important to me?”

OUSS: (chuckling) “Sure, go for it! I’m set to start writing.”

Me: “I’m calling today to thank the Senator for co-sponsoring S.851 in the U.S. Senate. This bill addresses workplace violence prevention in healthcare and social services. I strongly feel that this legislation is very important. I am a nurse and a survivor of a violent patient assault that occurred while I was on duty. My son is a physician and my daughter a social worker. All of our professions are high risk for experiencing violence in the workplace according to the U.S. Bureau of Labor statistics. How was that?”

OUSS: “Perfect. I have it all written down and it is almost ready to be on the way to your Senator. I just need to add in your address and best contact information."

Me: "Before we hang up, the cynic in me needs to ask just one more question. Does it make any difference to call or write? Honestly?"

OUSS: "Honestly? Yes. It does make a difference. When we hear from people, the issue definitely shows up on her radar. When we hear from multiple people, it gains even more of her attention."

***

Using the information that you wrote down at the start of this portion of your bullet journal, forge ahead with the next part.

Who are the elected officials that are in a position to either write or support legislation regarding this issue? Depending on what the concern is, you may want to explore contacting someone at the local, state, or federal levels.

•

•

•

Fill in your SBAR template.

Situation:

Background:

Assessment:

Recommendation:

Now, write that letter or email. Be sure to proofread the final product and then send it off! Congratulations, you are finding your voice!

Chapter 17:

*Rosie, RN**

"If I ever find you, and I will, I will slit your throat and watch you bleed to death, you fucking bitch."
~ PACU patient to Rosie

As I finished the interviews with the survivors of healthcare workplace violence included in this book, I was struck by the realization that my soul was thirsty for the story of someone who could talk about what had helped him, her, or them to heal. I was gasping like a fish out of water, to be quite honest, realizing it was a missing element. Utilizing the tentacles of social media, I began my search for someone willing to tell their story of healing which I so longed to hear. Almost immediately, Rosie reached out to share her message.

It's easy to become overwhelmed and stuck in a sense of hopelessness after hearing the narratives of healthcare workers who have lived through violence in the workplace. The seemingly endless shockwaves that violence sends through the lives of healthcare workers are daunting. At times, it feels as though there is no breakwater to slow the rush of those waves heading to shore.

I found that Rosie's story was no different from so many others in the way it began. The epilogue to her story of workplace violence has given me hope, though.

I live in rural New England. Stone walls dot the local landscape in this area and property boundaries are often defined by them. These stalwart remnants of the past are a testimony to our heritage. They are also the tangible legacies of those who worked hard to scratch out an existence here in the past. Long after the people who built those stone walls are gone, the product of their labors remain. Healthcare workers, like my forefathers and mothers, also leave a lasting imprint on the world. Patients, families, and co-workers, however, may become distant memories over the decades of a life of hard work. As the years pass, what becomes a blur for the healer may remain an intricate memory for the one who received care.

A legacy may not even rise to the surface of consciousness for some; think of the housekeeper who spends years diligently cleaning and organizing a patient care area. That housekeeper provided a safe environment for healing.

Rosie spoke lovingly of her patients and the time spent caring for them. Over the years, she has worked hard to attain the education, skill, and experience to care for postoperative patients in the Post Anesthesia Care Unit (PACU). She was quick to frame her legacy in nursing as that of providing competent, compassionate care to patients and their families.

It is not unusual to hear individual stories that all contain a similar theme after a violent episode occurs in healthcare. The common thread involves recounting a chronicle of workplace violence, horror being expressed, and then... often, there is a blunt amputation, and silence. The situation has been controlled. The plane has crashed and is no longer on the radar screen. The wreckage is out of sight. The easiest resolution of the problem involves eliminating from the workplace any reminders of the event. Time for the next big story to move to the forefront of communal awareness. Utilizing this technique for damage control serves the industry well, but it does not serve the workers. There is no problem if the existence of workplace violence is not acknowledged, right? If there is no problem, why would a solution be needed? This all feels a little like the toddler who is "hiding" from you by covering his eyes... he can't see you so you, obviously, cannot see him either.

And then, the game can just go on. But we are not toddlers. And the game is frighteningly real and pervasive. So, what about that blunt amputation? What does that look and feel like? What is the work that has to be done to get back up and walking after this figurative dismembering occurs? The goal of this chapter is to focus on Rosie's healing, but I would be doing her a major disservice if I didn't give a synopsis of the event that caused the injury.

A couple of salient points assist in painting the background to set the scene for what happened to Rosie on one Sunday a few years ago. The elements that must be examined are: 1) the policy of mandating certain specialty nursing areas to take "call," and 2) what the specialty practice of post anesthesia nursing entails.

Specialty areas of nursing, such as the operating room and post-anesthesia care, are "open for business" during established hours in most institutions. These set hours allow for planning and executing a smooth and, potentially, lucrative business practice. This is achieved by scheduling and performing surgeries, stabilizing patients in the Post Anesthesia Care Unit (PACU), and sending them either home or on to designated patient care units for further care. While a surgical procedure may be considered "routine" or minimal by a patient, the wild card for many is the anesthesia process. Going to sleep (anesthesia induction) and waking up (emergence) has been compared to the takeoff and landing of a commercial airline jet... the most dangerous parts of the flight.

PACU nurses are skilled in assessment, pain management, and resolving medical emergencies. Patients must meet specific criteria for discharge before they can leave PACU.

The same facilities that work to tweak the raw materials of the operating room and PACU into revenue sources, are quite often faced with being open to accommodate urgent/emergent cases during off hours. To meet the need to be available 24/7, some institutions require both perioperative and PACU nurses to take "call." This means assigning shifts to staff members, in addition to their regular work hours, to be available to go to work when needed based on patient-care demands. We used to joke that call could be defined as spending your day off working for exceptionally small pay while hitched to a very short leash. Many in the profession do not savor this work requirement and the resulting effect on their personal lives.

Rosie's story of violence occurred on a Sunday while she was on call for PACU at a 250-bed community hospital that is part of a large medical conglomerate. As with many untoward events, violence occurs when a series of small, seemingly insignificant, bits of flotsam bubble to the surface, allowing the maelstrom of a stinking mess to suddenly evolve.

Rosie accepted the transfer of a patient to the PACU from the operating room. In report, there was only the slightest foreshadowing of the challenges to arrive in the near future. The only hint that there might be difficulties managing the patient was given in the report when the anesthesiologist stated, "This guy has been abusing his body his entire life, and now he is pissed off about it."

Not long after the hand-off, sure enough, the patient became disruptive and started pulling critical monitors off. Rosie attempted to calm him. In the midst of stabilizing him, the patient stopped responding to verbal stimuli. Concerned for the patient's well-being, Rosie expanded her approach to rouse him by utilizing a common technique known as a glabellar tap (a tap on the forehead above the eyes), he was suddenly alert and very, very angry. The now responsive patient offered, "If you do that again, I will kick the shit out of you."

Rosie documented this threat in the patient record. The dust of the situation seemed to settle, but it had stirred up Rosie's gut instinct and she was more than a little concerned about her safety in the isolated PACU area. The patient became quiet. Rosie's intuition, though, told her that the disruptive behavior was far from over; she had the feeling that the patient was rather like a silent snake, coiled and waiting to strike. Shortly after this confrontation, Rosie located assistance to transfer the patient safely up to his assigned space in the Intensive Care Unit.

The story doesn't end yet, though. While handing off the patient and giving report to the nurses on the unit, the patient became "unresponsive" once again. Rosie described the cascade of events that followed in almost clinical detail:

"It was there he started pulling off monitors—slowly and deliberately with his eyes closed—and hiding the pulse ox[imeter] under his hip (he was on his side) so we didn't have a good monitor reading on him. I told the ICU nurses, 'he is fine, this is what he does.' They insisted I get a verbal response from him, so after saying his name and jostling him a little, I tapped him on the forehead, forgetting his previous threat. That's when he woke up, sat up, and leaned forward. I had moved to his feet. He started calling me everything but a white woman, and tugging on my sleeve, and at that point (the ONLY time in my career I had on one of those paper OR jackets) I tore off the sleeve. He fell back and I stepped away."

Then the patient looked at Rosie and said, "If I ever find you, and I will, I will slit your throat and watch you bleed to death, you fucking bitch."

Hospital security soon arrived on the scene. Police were called. Rosie made a statement regarding the physical and verbal assault, but declined to press charges. Interestingly enough, the patient demanded to press charges AGAINST Rosie. The police officers denied his request. Remarkably, Rosie wasn't injured. The work of the day continued on.

On a Friday, three months after the incident, Rosie was asked to step into the manager's office. She was met by representatives of the nursing, administration, and legal departments. During this meeting, she was presented with an eight-page letter detailing "research" into the situation. Apparently, the patient was not happy and felt that his rights had been infringed upon by Rosie while she was following PACU protocols to deliver safe care. Her own documentation of his threats toward her helped the nursing management and legal office to make the case for Rosie's suspension from duty. The issues of his verbal threats and physical assault were not of interest to the management. What was of critical importance was strategically removing some source of the patient's unhappiness. Rosie found herself suspended and being escorted out of the building in tears after the meeting. The following Tuesday, Rosie received a phone call to let her know that she was terminated from employment at the hospital.

What about the co-workers who watched as Rosie was escorted out on that horrible day? After all, this drama played out in front of her colleagues. The next part of the amputation procedure involved making sure that Rosie did not have contact with any of the current employees of the facility. Management clearly dictated that there was to be absolutely no contact with Rosie. Without understanding the whole background for Rosie's termination, the door was opened to allow imaginations to run wild with fear and uncertainty.

Remember, for this amputation to be a success, it was key to not let Rosie tell anyone in the workplace her story. By not airing this "dirty laundry," the medical conglomerate hoped to accomplish the goal of quickly regaining its equilibrium without accepting any responsibility or accountability for the violence in the workplace. There was no need to make any changes in safety or patient care practices. Concierge health delivery was safe for another day. Damage control at its finest, right? And for Rosie? No opportunity to tell her story. No chance of receiving support. No closure after thirteen years of employment. And, just like that, the problem for the business was solved. Rosie and her co-workers had just suffered an assault... this time at the hands of their employer.

I was truly gobsmacked by this story. I thought to myself, "How do you come back from this?" Rosie is resourceful and realistic. She offered that much of the healing happened "from the inside out." Rosie has a deep and abiding faith, which has kept her afloat during this difficult time. That same faith helped her to feel far less alone as she was unceremoniously removed from the building and left to face an uncertain professional future. Fortunately, she has also developed a core group of nursing colleagues who have become good friends over the years. One, in particular, took the risk to reach out and spend time with Rosie on the day of her dismissal. Brave and loyal friends are miraculous, life-affirming additions to the foxholes of the healthcare workplace. Rosie was blessed with nurses who stepped in to provide support and encouragement. This circle of friendship allowed Rosie the space and grace to start healing from both the patient assault and the trauma of being fired.

One of the lifelines that Rosie clung to on the day of her suspension sparks a little feeling of joy in my heart. As she explained to me, Rosie had previously made plans with a buddy to go to a 'paint with a twist' class to be held on the evening of the Friday that she was suspended. Safe to say, Rosie wasn't feeling much like painting or socializing after the soul sucking events on what would end up being the last day at her job. Rosie's friend dug her heels in and insisted that they continue with the plans to attend the painting class. Such a simple outing, but it gave Rosie the opportunity to take a breath and have a little taste of joy from reconnecting with something that made her happy. Rosie had a break to just be her wonderful self, not defined by the life-changing events of the day.

Rosie summed up her thoughts about moving forward. In her own words: "I love my patients, but I am so tired of the bullshit. I have accepted that this [experience] is just the reality of working in an 'industry.' In all honesty, I've come to realize that the job was really pretty horrible in a lot of ways. I was lucky because the actual impact of the violence could have been so much worse."

After hearing the acceptance and resolution in Rosie's voice, I believe that we need to add those uncompromising strengths to the legacy of her nursing career. The "industry" is broken, but it has certainly not broken Rosie. Healing has taken place, but at what cost and to what end?

*Name changed at interviewee's request for anonymity.

Addendum: Rosie is once again working in a new and very different practice area from PACU. She is excited to learn new skills and to have returned to caring for patients. Her own healing continues.

Chapter 18:

First Aid

What do we think of when we hear the expression "first aid?" It brings images of someone who may have little or no actual medical training providing the care needed to assist a person immediately after an injury has occurred. First aid is an interim activity meant to tide the patient over until a more concerted effort from trained professionals is available. The beauty of receiving first aid cannot be overstated. Well given first aid can stop an injury from becoming worse and has been known to be lifesaving.

Hardly a home, purse, or car doesn't have some sort of first aid kit tucked away for sudden injuries. Much better to be prepared with some basic supplies than to be caught short without them. You really just never know what might come in handy. Over the years, I have stored away the debris left over from a variety of small and large injuries suffered by my offspring (mostly my son, if I'm honest). You just never know when some bit of this detritus could turn a situation around and save the day. I must have learned this hoarding behavior from my mother, another nurse. When I was tasked with cleaning my parents' house out prior to selling it, I found a plethora of partially used prescriptions and medical supplies gathered over the fifty-plus years that they lived there. One of the most interesting finds was a little brown bottle with an eyedropper cover.

This gem dated back to the 1960's and sported a label from a long-defunct pharmacy in a nearby town. It contained the medication 'tincture of opium,' and the directions were given for dosing a bad case of diarrhea. I am quite sure that some of the items that she had stored away were no longer approved for human use and probably more appropriate for a display on the history of medicine in a natural science museum.

What I am interested in sharing in this final chapter involves a different sort of first aid kit. It encompasses emotional and spiritual first aid. More about that in a moment; first I need to state the obvious regarding my notion about immediate care for physical injuries. Here is the statement to mull over: depending on what sort of violence has occurred, it is key to acknowledge physical injuries and to render physical first aid if needed–real first aid that you may remember from your days in Boy Scouts or Girl Scouts. I understand that it seems more than a little idiotic to make the assertion that healthcare professionals and medical facilities need to respond to physical injuries when a member of their workforce has been assaulted; perhaps we all have assumed that this is the routine protocol when a staff member has been the victim of physical violence. But assumptions get us into trouble around basic issues and I do not want to condone that continuing to happen in the future.

So, I will say it clearly: if you or a colleague have been physically injured by violence in the workplace, you deserve to receive thorough and competent assessment of—and treatment for—those injuries. This care needs to be delivered by healthcare professionals. It is not appropriate to expect an injured person to triage their own status and determine a plan of care for themselves.

As I listen to the stories of injured workers, it has become apparent that, for many of the people I have interviewed for this book, attending to their physical injuries was haphazard, at best. I cannot begin to understand the justification for not calling an ambulance for a healthcare worker seriously injured in a physical assault, but it happens. When someone has been assaulted in the healthcare workplace, they have the right to care and concern for each and every one of their injuries; physical, emotional, and spiritual.

As I gathered information for this book, I incorporated a question for all of the people I interviewed: "If we were constructing a first aid kit for people who have experienced violence in the healthcare workplace, what item would you like to make sure it contained?"

The first time that I voiced the inquiry, I was met with absolute silence. Nothing. And, then, there was a hesitant response. It seems that nobody had ever asked that question before. It was befuddling to be asked what could make a positive difference for the survivors. Or, for the survivors with whom I spoke, it was more than a little disorienting to frame a response to the query. No one else had asked what would have served them better after being assaulted. No one had asked them what they had needed in order to heal. It was tentatively suggested that it might be easier if I could re-work the order of the interview and consider mentioning this question in the beginning of our conversation, enabling the interviewee time to get their head wrapped around the notion that they were in the driver's seat to make a recommendation for a positive change based on their personal experience.

I guess that you could call it a case of empowering the victims to make a tiny step forward, shifting the culture of how they were treated post violence. I took the suggestion to heart and found that, after initiating a bit of fine tuning with my interview technique, the responses I received in future interactions were often quite breathtaking.

Like a good first aid kit, it is key to have resources in order and easily locatable when needed. The most organized way for this to happen is to have everything in one designated place so that it can be readily accessed. Who wants to look in the bottom of the kitchen catch-all drawer for something to use as a tourniquet when you or your loved one is spurting arterial blood? Having resources well-organized in an institutional setting can be tricky, especially when that institution is invested in not acknowledging the need for them.

As mentioned previously, there are institutions beginning to address the importance of providing support to the staff during what may seem like insurmountable challenges. Cleveland Clinic, an academic medical center located in Cleveland, Ohio, has initiated a response called Code Lavender. Code Lavender is activated when an untoward event has impacted the staff in a patient-care area. For example, it may be called when there has been a mass casualty event, such as a school shooting with victims being brought to the local hospital for treatment. Or, a Code Lavender may be called when there is an unexpected death of a patient or staff member. This is an organized, holistic approach to support the staff during and after a crisis in the workplace. Part of this response consists of bolstering the staffing numbers with competent caregivers so that the affected staff members are able to fully engage in the support offered.

I believe that shifts in culture may happen incrementally. Changes start with one conversation at a time, yet initiating those conversations may seem impossible. I remind you about the foundational concept which was shared in an earlier chapter that we have to acknowledge a painful situation, along with its accompanying emotions, for healing to begin.

Before Code Lavender could be born, the need for and benefits of staff support during extremely challenging situations had to be recognized. Someone had to open the door to allow the conversation that would start the ball rolling.

The first and second items in our first aid kit, while being packed by two different people, go together like pieces of a very expensive jigsaw puzzle. You know the ones that I mean, the puzzles that have pieces that are seamless in the way that they connect and fit together. As our interview began to wind down, I asked Chaplain Joe Perez what he would pack in a first aid kit for a recent victim of violence. He approached the answer from an unexpected angle with a suggestion that took me completely by surprise.

Joe began his response by circling in on a feeling that he would like to pack. Words to boil down the description of what he was reaching for were elusive at first. I could almost hear a smile in Joe's voice when he suggested an example of what he wanted to pack – the feeling that an emotional therapy dog brings to a difficult situation. In my mind, I was picturing those big, furry bundles known as Golden Retrievers, leaning up against someone who has just weathered a tragedy. That visual allowed Joe to expand on this first aid supply. He offered that he would pack the sense of calmness achieved when a therapy dog steps into an emotionally uncomfortable situation. This soft, gentle creature provides a wordless, compassionate presence that allows a supportive connection so organic that it is almost magical.

Comfort and strength may be found simply in being accompanied by the four-legged bundle of fuzzy warmth on that first tenuous step of the healing journey. More about this first aid supply in a bit. First, let's think about a bit of preparatory work to help arrange a sound environment to promote a healing situation. This work could be compared to washing our hands and putting gloves on before attempting to dress a nasty wound. Taking care of ourselves helps us to safely care for others.

We all have the potential to be that calm presence for another. How do we start to incorporate the use of this piece of the first aid kit that Joe included? Here comes the other puzzle piece that I mentioned earlier. I suggest that you consider starting with a survey of your own self. Included in this survey are your thoughts, feelings, and emotions around the troubling issue of violence in the healthcare workplace.

Heather Plett, when asked what she would include in the first aid kit for healthcare workers who have experienced violence, tucked in the idea of supporting liminal space. Take a breath, and another, and admit that there are times when we just have to purposefully wade through the ugliness. Sometimes, after an overwhelming event, we simply need to allow time to be in that uncomfortable space of the feelings caused by what we have just experienced. No lecture or advice required. How does that feel? You don't always have to have an answer or a plan to fix a situation. Look around that swamp full of raw feelings and allow them to exist. Get to know them. By allowing yourself this time to become familiar with all of the feelings and emotions around an event, you open the door so that you may step over the threshold into a new space. Heather Plett offers that this process allows you to move forward in a transformative journey rather than being imprisoned by the denial of discomfort, which locks you into the old story playing forever on a blistering endless loop. That old narrative not only traps you in the swamp, but it also enables you to be comfortable wearing blinders to ignore others struggling in the mire.

Give yourself permission to drop the warrior mentality of perpetual strength and knowledge and embrace your own vulnerability. As you reach the other side of the swamp, Heather offers that your perspective may shift, and you may find this shift quite freeing; you may even discover that you have changed in how you view the world. The old warrior approach of bucking up, soldiering on, and stepping over a painful emotional morass may have given way to a new sense of compassion and empathy for both yourself and others swimming in the sea of healthcare violence.

I highly recommend looking at Heather Plett's website, https://heatherplett.com/holdingspace/, to explore her writings more fully.

Please take a moment to recall the story that I previously recounted of the medical student who was verbally assaulted in the nurses' station by the angry ward clerk. I can still picture the embarrassment, humiliation, and horror on his face. I can also see the clerk's face contorted in anger as she hissed her vitriolic words at him.

Do I believe that this was a life-altering event for either of them? Perhaps, but that's hard to know at this point. Did the aggressive behavior of the ward clerk toward students continue unchecked? Did the medical student begin to learn that it was permissible to behave disrespectfully to people holding "lower status" in the medical hierarchy? I wonder if either took time to sit down and process what happened that day. How did that aggressive communication impact the rest of their day? Did it affect their interactions with patients, staff, or teachers? Did it affect how they felt about themselves?

Hypothetically, if any reflection on the event did occur, what do you suppose was the conclusion? Did either of the participants feel the need to make changes in how they navigated the world as they came out on the other side of the emotional morass full of the ugliness of anger and verbal violence? Doing this work could have been quite life-altering and even a little liberating for both participants in this painful interaction. Those uncomfortable emotions may have transformed into something quite different. They may have even sprouted the wings of empathy and compassion.

Giving yourself permission and space to become comfortable with spending time in that liminal emotional space described so eloquently by Heather Plett will aid in putting Joe's suggestion into practice. Let's return to the notion of channeling the calm presence of an emotional therapy dog. How can we use this supply in the first aid kit to help those around us?

I think that we can start by taking a page from Joe's playbook; stop talking and *listen*. When someone is fresh from a traumatic incident, just be present. Many of us are hard wired to "fix" a perceived problem. Everything will straighten back out if we just check all the boxes on the list and move on. Algorithms are beautiful action-oriented plans. The next step needed to resolve a situation is readily determined by the presence or absence of a symptom; if this is present, then that is indicated. As the limbs of the algorithm build, so do the activities. Rarely do we find a leg of an algorithm that recommends simply being present for the pain and suffering as the prescribed action. Channeling your inner therapy dog may be a struggle, but what this means is there is no need to offer solutions or judge the person's response to the situation.

Remember, dogs don't have opposing digits so they are hindered from acting on a lot of the "fixes" that humans tend to embrace.

Refrain from making assumptions about the impact of the situation. Trauma affects everyone differently, and pep talks are not required. Take the first step and give it a try. Is one of your colleagues or a student looking stressed with what the day has delivered? Engage with them. Pour them a cup of coffee when you pour yourself one. Ask how they are and listen to the answer. Acknowledge and validate what is offered. Be aware that the day may have given them a literal or figurative slap in the face. Validate the belief that some days are difficult and challenging.

As you recall, there is no need to fix or organize a solution. Allow yourself the sacred privilege of providing a safe, calming presence to another; that non-judgmental, compassionate, wet-nosed, pile of furriness. You don't have to solve a situation, just to open the door so that the colleague may feel safe and comfortable in acknowledging that the challenge exists. You have just given them a branch to grasp while navigating the gooey, brown bits of the swamp that they are navigating. The good news is that they are no longer all alone in the muck. They may feel a lot better simply because you listened and supported them.

Rosie offered the inclusion of a first aid supply, which some areas may already use after an episode of violence in the workplace: debriefing. Many of us have heard of and/or practiced debriefing in the workplace. I have been part of debriefing sessions after challenging surgical procedures. Usually, all of the participants in an event gather together at the end to discuss what went well, what could have gone better, and what changes could be made to incorporate improvements in the future.

Rosie unpacked the notion of debriefing, viewing it through a filter that lends the process to supporting the process of healing.

What Rosie envisioned involved a staff debriefing process which would take place immediately after an episode of violence; a designated time to focus on the needs of all those who experienced the violence—both victims and witnesses. Relieving the staff of patient-care responsibilities is a key stone of Rosie's suggestion for debriefing, so her protocol would allow the staff time to collect themselves while unpacking their thoughts and ideas around what had just occurred. She described mindfully examining what had just happened, without turning the process into one for agency quality assurance purposes. Supporting staff, not blaming or shaming. Rosie felt that a key element of this process must be an underlying commitment to grow a work culture that protects, values, and supports healthcare workers.

Glenda included a first aid supply, which paired effectively with Rosie's suggestion. After her experience of being threatened and assaulted by a patient, Glenda experienced isolation in her workplace. Isolation can be crippling. Post-violence, many victims offered that they were thrust into the shame/blame cycle, often feeling this start even before injuries were assessed. This echoing feeling of isolation can also lead to feelings of a punishing disconnection while amplifying the endless shame/blame loop. Multiple times, it was pointed out that the first question asked was, "What could you have done differently to prevent this from happening?" I asked Glenda what she would like to pack into the first aid kit, and she didn't hesitate with her answer. Glenda offered that she would pack a support system that would move in right after an episode of violence. There was solidness in her opinion. This support system would need to be committed to having a distinct focus on the needs of staff. Laser focused. This would not be a response created to simply check a box and to say that it exists. Glenda could only see this being truly effective if it was implemented and evaluated, continually assessing whether it met the needs of those affected. While discussing this idea, I could feel the impetus behind Glenda's concern. Programs and services are "marketed," but may, by simply existing on paper and in committee, promote an undeserved sense of success at meeting the needs of those they are meant to serve. But something that exists merely on paper or in the computer of the management team serves no one. It is paying lip service to the law.

Glenda was critical of complacency within the healthcare system, justifiably so. She asserted that any support system working to assist the victim of healthcare workplace violence needed to be victim centered. She offered, "Don't ask the person to let you know if they need anything; ask the person what you can do for them at that moment."

The first aid item that Glenda described would be a dynamic entity, incorporating continuous assessment, planning, and evaluation, all critical parts of the nursing process to promote a positive outcome. A stagnant response plan could have little or no true value, according to Glenda.

Tina Suckow offered that the first aid item that she would include would be an organizational culture where the administration would support the injured worker rather than assign blame to the victims. She described a workplace that would treat all of the victims with "the same kindness, respect, and compassion that I had for my patients." What would that look like? A commitment to a safe workplace is key to laying the foundation for this metamorphosis. Leadership/management accepting a role in holding themselves accountable for the safety of those working or receiving care in an organization is a paramount first step to be taken. Listening to the experiences and first-hand knowledge of the frontline stakeholders would enable the administration to address more realistically the problem of workplace violence. This step is tricky because it involves simultaneously admitting to the broken bits of the system while working to build trust with staff.

Unfortunately, as most of us are aware, without trust, authenticity and honesty wither and die.

Acknowledging the existence and severity of workplace violence requires the "industry" to step into some vulnerability, to show that it knows its own faults and failings, and that it wishes to improve. The polish of the business plan becomes scratched and tarnished when the marketing façade cracks to openly show the ugliness of healthcare workplace violence. Stark reality can be unpalatable fodder for the public relations of the healthcare industry. Tina was quick to point out that a healthcare organization well-grounded in integrity and commitment to its staff would enable the existence of a new sort of managerial value system. This shift in philosophy would support accommodating the staff injured while on duty, rather than dispensing with them. Even if unable to return to their former employment positions, these staff members would continue to be valuable and productive in the organization, shifting into another role. As such, then, they would not end up feeling punished for something that was not their fault in the first place.

The first aid kit is starting to have an interesting composition, isn't it? The list of items described thus far could serve everyone working in healthcare well, not just victims of workplace violence. All of what has been packed in the first aid kit would serve the victims of all violence whether it is vertical, lateral, verbal, or physical. Some, such as Heather Plett's suggestion, might even prevent some acts of violence from occurring. If the wounded healer were to recognize their injuries and work to regain a sense of health, perhaps incidents of lashing out using lateral violence in healthcare would decrease.

Before I continue with other items so graciously suggested to me by the contributors to this book, let's take a little break. I am interested in turning the focus over to you, the reader. I have included a few prompts that I hope will open up the door to reflecting on what you might think is imperative to pack in a first aid kit for yourself and for others. My wish for you is that it will add an extra dimension to this chapter that you may choose to incorporate into your daily life.

Bullet Journal #12

From what you have read so far in this chapter, what "first aid supply" would be a good thing to have available in your work life?

For yourself?

•

For co-workers?

•

In which recent situations would you have found an emotional first aid kit helpful?

•

•

•

What is the first aid supply you would have liked to have had available after experiencing workplace violence, either as the victim or as a witness?

In what ways would you start to incorporate this first aid supply into your life?

-
-
-

Have you been the victim of lateral or vertical violence?

What three emotions come up after experiencing lateral or vertical violence?

-
-
-

Give yourself space to think back and reflect on when you participated in perpetrating lateral or vertical violence. Without excusing or justifying your actions, what were the emotions (that you felt at the time) which supported this behavior?

-
-
-

What were the intentions of your actions? Honestly.

-
-

What feelings fueled the idea that you were justified in participating in lateral or vertical violence?

-
-
-

Name three emotions you would feel if the same violence were to be perpetrated against you.

-
-
-

List two thoughts that come up for you after doing this reflection.

-
-

On a scale of 1-10, with 1 being "absent" and 10 being "can totally put myself in the other person's shoes," how would you rate your capacity for empathy in the workplace?

Name three behaviors that, in the recent past, demonstrated your ability to empathize with someone (other than a patient or client) in your workplace.

-
-
-

Without thinking too long, list four words that describe how you feel when you are in a stressful situation and someone empathizes with you.

-
-
-
-

Extra credit:

Do you work in an environment where you interact with students? Perhaps medical students? Take a look at the book, Human Voices of Tomorrow's Doctors, edited by Tolu Kehinde. Read some of the stories and give yourself a few moments to reflect on the perspective of the authors.

Write a sentence describing your thoughts about empathizing with the authors of the stories that you read.

Name four shifts that have occurred in your perspective about medical students.

-
-
-
-

Think about how these shifts will impact your interactions with medical students in the future. Name two changes that you will make.

-

-

Back to packing the first aid kit... DJ inserted "strength, peace, grounding which comes from a sense of not being alone." Simple, but fiercely powerful words for us to tuck into our souls. Think about some of the most unnerving times in your life; what did you long to have? DJ's words resonated with me in a striking way; I never really understood what alone truly was until I regained consciousness from being assaulted. People were around, but I was so alone. I woke up on that floor all by myself, and thought that I was dead. Never again will I underestimate the potentially terrifying impact of finding myself alone in a situation. Our strength is multiplied algebraically when we aren't standing on our own.

The roots of a tree provide it with stability, nourishment, and a foundation, so that it may remain upright and grow tall. Grounding gives us the invisible roots allowing us to feel powerful enough to venture into the unknown, where we don't know what the outcome will be. I leave this first aid item up for the reader's personal interpretation. Some may find it in a deeply rooted faith. Others may collect bits along the way from those who have mentored and supported them. Coworkers, friends, and family may be what creates this net. Whatever the line is which ties you to this anchor of graceful connectedness, it will require some attention and care. You need to focus and cultivate what grounds you and gives you strength and peace. Relationships do not just happen. Even when you find what is important to you, please don't take it for granted and allow it to languish.

When trying to pack this first aid item, please remember that it is a bit like a falling star; it is beautiful to watch, but you really need to pay attention when it is happening or you will miss it. Unashamedly and unapologetically, connect with who and what feeds your spirit. Accept that those around you may spin their web of grounding and connection differently, and that the differences may even be quite beautiful if viewed in their uniqueness. Hold that thought, please, since it sets the stage for the next item in the first aid jump kit.

Hannah spoke not only of living through the physical and verbal violence directed at her by patients, but also of the effects of lateral violence within the nursing profession. Her willingness to embrace both the bitter and the sweet aspects of her injuries and scars allowed for her to offer an interesting first aid supply. This may be used with success both prophylactically as well as therapeutically in a violent healthcare workplace. If you think about it, people who provide care to clients and patients are very much like the individual pieces of that gorgeous, expensive jigsaw puzzle to which I alluded earlier. Each piece is nice and unique, but together, when assembled with all the parts meshing correctly, the end result becomes a clear, vibrant picture. This lovely final result would not exist if all of the pieces were exactly the same shape with precisely the same design placed on them; you would simply have a pile of cardboard cutouts. Hannah's words in response to my question of what first aid supply she would pack still take my breath away as I write them here. She quietly said, "The capacity to stop and ponder the other person's story; the messy and beautiful parts that got me where I am today, aren't the same messy and beautiful parts that got you where you are today."

Just imagine if we all started to utilize this first aid supply right now, replacing judgment and assumptions with curiosity. What would happen? It may sound a bit optimistic, but I could certainly see a much healthier, richer culture take root. At the end of the day, I wonder if perhaps even a few lives of healthcare workers might be saved.

You may be wondering what I would pack in the first aid kit. I would pack the sense of value that each of you brings to healing. Your value and worth is independent of the opinions of others and not to be determined by them. You are priceless. NO "bottom line" on the revenue sheet can compute your worth in the healthcare industry. You cannot be replaced because there is only one YOU. What you bring as a healer to the intricate ballet known as healthcare is magical and unique. You may never even know just how incredibly valuable it is. Your imprint may seem to be invisible or opaque, but it exists for whoever you touched along the way. You all deserve a workplace that enables and allows you to excel and a culture that provides you the very, very best—safety, support, compassion, and a place to thrive as a healer. You are deserving.

Things to consider…

If you are supporting someone immediately after an episode of workplace violence:

- Don't assume that the person wants to be left alone.

- Ask what is needed specifically such as food, a ride to an appointment, childcare, etc.

- Don't offer advice or lectures. Platitudes aren't terribly helpful either.

- Show up and be present. Don't isolate the person.

- Resist the temptation to ask, "What's the plan?" The person may not know what is happening next and has no plan figured out. This is uncharted territory. The workplace, which once was the source of a victim's financial support, may now be hostile. The profession providing a big part of their identity may no longer be an option for the future. Asking about the "plan" may only ramp up the victim's anxiety. Stay in the moment.

- Avoid asking questions that smack of Monday morning quarterbacking. Let the victim get through their own process without asking "what could you have done differently" or offering what you would have done in the situation. This line of discussion doesn't help anything, but it does open the door to shame, blame, and guilt. This line of questioning also shuts the door to allowing the victim of violence to be vulnerable in sharing their thoughts and feelings with you in the future. They may only remember you as the person who grilled them with uncomfortable questions, and they may never wish to confide in you again.

- This suggestion seems basic, but bears sharing. Do not joke about the incident or injuries unless this is instigated by the victim. Similarly, do not laugh or minimize the situation. While this may help you with your discomfort around the topic, it may be perceived very differently by the victim.

- Practice your sense of empathy. Put yourself in the other person's shoes for a moment.

- Allow the person to verbalize their feelings and emotions without criticizing what they are expressing.

- Give the person space and leeway for good days and bad days. Healing is not linear, so they may be "up" one day and down the next; this doesn't mean a thing, except that they are processing things. Don't assume that you know how they are feeling without asking. If they are struggling, quiet, reticent, and unsociable, don't take it personally.

- Try to refrain from sharing information that you have heard from the victim unless you have permission to do so. Respect their privacy and their journey. If others ask you to divulge information, offer that they should speak directly to the victim. It isn't your story to either tell, talk about, or critique.

- Avoid the temptation to "fix" problems for the victim. Don't offer advice unless specifically asked by the victim.

You may discover other new and different ideas about first aid supplies which you plan to pack in your own kit. I hope that you do and that you not only use them, but also share them with others.

None of us can go back and rewrite the beginning of our experience with healthcare workplace violence. It is history. We do have the power to purposefully change the ending of our stories; and, the stories of others.

Chapter 19:

Hope

I am looking back at the progression through this book and now realize that there is one topic that deserves its very own space: hope. Living through the experience of violence, and surviving it, requires a great deal of hope. At first, I fell into the trap of thinking that following the path of least resistance required me to give up and accept the status quo. As someone once told me several months after the assault, I looked as though I was on the way to become one of those old folks who passed the days sitting on a park bench, feeding the ducks, and simply waiting to die.

This was a fairly accurate description; I had given up.

Back in nursing school, I had a particularly aggravating instructor on the pediatric and maternal-infant rotations. She had a saying that was shared fast and frequently in a variety of challenging situations, "Where there's life, there's hope." In my younger, less seasoned days of nursing, I thought that this was a totally asinine philosophy. Then came Lynne Truxillo. Lynne's experience made me sit up and pay attention to an asset I had been remiss in embracing: life. I am alive, and there is hope.

What does that hope feel like? I liken feeling hopeful to heading into a busy traffic roundabout. You know that your exit is there, but the situation requires a certain amount of faith and diligence to navigate the traffic while keeping your eyes open for the turn that will take you in your desired direction. Even if it takes a couple of passes around the traffic circle, you just know that eventually, the path will open up and you will be purposefully traveling on it. Hope does not guarantee an easy journey. It does offer the prospect of potential. The awareness of the possibility for finding the route to a desired outcome. Hope is what allows us to get off that park bench, leave the ducks to go on about their business, and regain the determination to open the door to meaningful change.

I have learned that even the tiniest of changes in behaviors and attitudes, if acknowledged, may affirm positive progress. If you have made it this far in your reading, you have quite possibly experienced some realignment in your thoughts and previously held beliefs. You may also have started to establish some healthy boundaries regarding formerly accepted behaviors of others. If you are the survivor of a violent assault, you may be doing the challenging work of acknowledging your feelings and emotions around what happened to you and the impact it has left. Perhaps reading this book has helped you to feel supported and strong so that you may continue with your healing. Proper respect to you for this! Please know that, just as the flutter of the butterfly's wings on one side of the world may cause a windstorm on the other side, you are causing a shift in the universe of not only your life, but also in the lives of peers and patients. Just as the wind increases with each flutter of delicate wings, your behaviors and ideas will gain momentum and grow. I believe that, like the energetic little butterfly, you may not see the full results of your efforts in the bigger picture. But you are making an impact. Have hope.

Epilogue

I began this book just ahead of the start of the COVID-19 pandemic. While I felt called to put my thoughts on paper about what assists in the healing process after experiencing violence in the healthcare workplace, my impetus took a nose dive as the pandemic reared its ugly head.

After all, who really could possibly care about healthcare workers being assaulted when thousands and thousands of people were sick and dying? And, then, the horror stories about the lack of personal protective equipment (PPE) started surfacing. Hot on the heels of those stories came the narratives about healthcare workers being assaulted because of wearing scrubs in public, or being threatened with firearms at the gas pump, or being hit by cars while working in drive-through testing centers, or spit on and threatened in hospitals.

And then, the healthcare workers started dying from COVID-19 infections. Yet in the middle of a global pandemic, the frontline "heroes" were still showing up to care for their patients in spite of the lack of PPE, exposure to a potentially fatal disease, politicizing of the public health disaster, and the aggression directed at them by the general public. By every account I have heard—and I have listened to many—care continued and continues to be delivered to the sick and dying with kindness and compassion.

As we slip into the end of our first year in this pandemic, I have arrived at the realization that we, the frontline workers, need support and space to heal more than ever. During the second half of this first year of this public health crisis, I have watched esteemed medical scientists being disregarded and threatened. Unemployment is rampant. Healthcare disparity between the "haves" and "have nots" has become an even larger gaping chasm than before the pandemic arrived on our doorstep. Businesses are closing their doors permanently. Hospital resources are taxed to the breaking point in some areas of the country. Many medical facilities are struggling to survive in the face of decreased revenues. Human resources in healthcare have been stretched so thinly that I sometimes wonder who will be left when this pandemic is finally under control. It is not uncommon to hear people casually speak about the health of the economy taking priority over the value of human lives. After all, people are going to die...

Yet, when questioned, those same folks expect the very best of first-world healthcare if they or their families are sick. They aren't quite as easy going about the effects of COVID-19 affecting them or their loved ones. And, to the dismay of many healthcare workers, there is a whole segment of the population that does not even believe that this pandemic exists or is a cause for concern. Our value of humanity and dignity has been challenged.

Take a look back at the chapter on the present state of healthcare, "I Think That the Tree is Dying." All of those factors were present BEFORE we were jettisoned into this public health battleground. From where I sit, frontline healthcare workers have become the present version of the soldiers who fought on the beaches of Normandy. Outmanned, outgunned, lacking protection, and no place to retreat, they can only shoulder their heavy packs and persevere in moving forward without drowning, regardless of the personal cost.

Recently, I asked a friend what she thought healthcare would look like after the dust of the pandemic settles. The reply was lovely in its naiveté. She offered, "Oh, I think that it will be a lot like it was before, except, perhaps a little better." Hmm, I wondered how that picture in her mind had come to be. Her answer was simple, "I think that we all deserve the very best healthcare services. I know that the people who sort out providing it believe the same thing; after all, that's just the way things are supposed to work in America, right?"

This notion, most likely shared by many consumers, may not actually coincide with the brutal reality of the shake-up that the COVID-19 pandemic has caused in the healthcare "industry." I believe that the after-shocks of the pandemic will be felt far into the future.

If I took a few snapshots of some of the not-so-publicized events that have impacted our healthcare forest during 2020, what would they look like? In the interest of being completely honest and authentic, I feel that it is my responsibility to share some of the album with you. This is not meant to discourage you from working to make changes, but rather to open your eyes and hearts to the emerging state of the healthcare forest as I see it. Always remember, we can only heal what we acknowledge.

Snapshot #1

As I discussed previously, in the U.S., many people rely on their places of employment to access health insurance coverage for themselves and their families. As the economy has struggled during the pandemic, many jobs have been lost. How many? It is estimated that roughly 5.4 million Americans lost their jobs and their health insurance between February and May of 2020. Sadly, this number exceeds all previous records held for the most adults becoming uninsured due to loss of employment in a single year.

Snapshot #2

Historically, jobs in healthcare have been considered a good option in terms of security and availability. The nursing profession has provided a great deal of career mobility and opportunities in the healthcare workforce. As time has gone on, each medical specialty has begun to require specific skill sets and training in order to provide safe and competent care. The pandemic caused a crisis within the healthcare forest when, suddenly, there was an emphasis on the high use of some roots – intensive care and emergency services, most especially. As hospitals attempted to make the shift to providing care to a large number of very ill COVID-19 infected patients, many of the routine medical procedures and care were put on hold in order to funnel resources where they were most needed. This shift resulted in a significant loss in necessary revenues from healthcare services; think about things like well-child visits or even routine colonoscopies. The decreased revenues resulted in the loss of 1.5 million healthcare jobs over the period of three months, February through April, in 2020. Thus, in an already "lean" industry, it is easy to imagine that the loss of these job positions will have a major impact on the delivery of healthcare services to consumers. I am willing to conjecture that while some jobs have returned, many of those 1.5 million healthcare positions are gone and we will not see them come back. If the jobs do return, where will those workers be? Surely, we can't expect them to wait around without income or health benefits until they can finally return to previously held positions. Many of those jobs were occupied by people at the low end of the pay scale in healthcare. While vital to providing services, living paycheck to paycheck in a job that has little or no security is not a tempting opportunity for many.

In another interesting side note, the numbers in this quote do not address the healthcare workers who have seen their work hours and income cut significantly, but still retain their jobs.

Snapshot #3

The final statistic is dark and foreboding for the future of healthcare delivery. We have all heard frontline healthcare workers referred to as "heroes" during these dark times. For many patients struck down by the novel coronavirus, their last link to humanity as they lay dying was with those healthcare professionals who cared for them. Healthcare workers diligently strived to save lives and assure dignified deaths for those who could not be saved; often with dwindling supplies and resources. The cost has been enormous. According to CDC statistics, at least 600 healthcare workers have died from COVID-19. The numbers of healthcare workers dying from COVID-19 increases daily. Some have argued that these statistics are skewed to the low end because of the strict definition and criteria used by the CDC to establish membership for the category of healthcare professional.

Many more frontline workers have been infected with the virus. While these individuals have survived the onslaught of the virus, for many, there has been little or no support from their workplaces. Here is an interesting point: claims made to Workers' Compensation have been overwhelmingly denied for those healthcare workers who have been sickened or died from COVID-19 infections. A fellow nurse cynically offered that we should not call the frontline healthcare workers "heroes," but should more appropriately refer to them as "sacrificial lambs."

Snapshot #4

Legislation, which was passed in the U.S. House of Representatives, went on to die in the U.S. Senate in the 2019-2020 session of Congress. This legislation would have opened the door to not only assessing the scope of healthcare workplace violence, but also holding employers accountable for implementing safety measures.

S. 851 Introduced in Senate (03/14/2019)

Workplace Violence Prevention for Healthcare and Social Service Workers Act

This bill requires the Department of Labor to address workplace violence in the healthcare and social service sectors. Specifically, Labor must promulgate an occupational safety and health standard that requires certain employers in the healthcare and social service sectors, as well as employers in sectors that conduct activities similar to the activities in the healthcare and social service sectors, to develop and implement a comprehensive plan for protecting healthcare workers, social service workers, and other personnel from workplace violence.

In addition, those employers must:

- investigate workplace violence incidents, risks, or hazards as soon as practicable;

- provide training and education to employees who may be exposed to workplace violence hazards and risks;

- meet record-keeping requirements;

- prohibit acts of discrimination or retaliation against employees for reporting workplace violence incidents, threats, or concerns.

No, I do not think that healthcare will be better when the pandemic is over. I believe that the potential healers of the future will look with horror at how this is playing out and, understandably, re-think any notion of joining the herd of sacrificial healthcare lambs. It is a hard sell to encourage the next generation to strive to gain admittance to a very competitive educational program, graduate with a mountain of debt, spend long hours in a highly dangerous environment, work under the shadow of polarized political whims, and have little job security or safety.

How do we turn this around? Where, oh where, do we start to stem this cascade of messiness before the entire system goes belly up? We, the healers on the ground floor, need to start acknowledging that we could use a little help here. We must regain our equilibrium and our sense of value to humanity. We need to look our own struggles in the eye, sit with them, and start healing.

Each and every one of us must commit to mindfully supporting each other, without judgment, during this process. We also need to admit that the way that we work together has broken bits, too. Putting energy into the manner in which we mesh in the healthcare space as interconnected puzzle pieces is key to regaining momentum to making our healing culture whole. Voices have to be raised and heard. Those in the leadership slots of the healthcare industry must spend time on the battlefront with the frontline workers. Listen to the stakeholders. Empower those who have the proverbial "skin in the game" to have a say in how their practices work and what healing environment works best for them and those they serve. What needs to be changed and what works well.

To those in elected offices, think about the future. Look at more than what will get you re-elected or maintain your spot in the partisan hierarchy. Open your ears and listen to what those who are the future healers have to say. Ask about what they see integral to their practices. Address disparity. Work on legislation allowing those who are struggling to get the help that they need. Honestly, look at the cost of committing to a medical education; is the student loan debt that healthcare workers carry realistic in today's world? Remember that healthcare will only be sustainable if you have people passionate about providing it.

And, what about the consumers of healthcare? Find your voices and raise them to advocate for yourselves and each other. You cannot expect anybody, ANYBODY, in this world to know what you want better than you do yourself. Trusting the "folks in charge" to do what you think is right on your behalf will only lead to disappointment if you do not learn to speak up and tell them your vision and goals. While you are speaking up, please remember that the people who provide you and those you love with care and comfort during your times of need are just that... people.

The healers deserve your support, advocacy, and understanding if they are to continue to care for patients/clients. They have a right to be safe while working in a healing environment. Above all, don't assume that they will always be there for you.

As one nurse offered, "Would I do this all over again? I don't know. I never wanted to work in an industry or on a production line, but here I am in the healthcare 'industry.' Folks think that this is a great job, but I'm just an hourly, blue-collar worker with mediocre benefits working at an "at will" position. I can be pretty much fired without any reason, so there's little job security. And the best part? I get to do this at all hours of the day and night plus weekends and holidays. I am exposed to deadly diseases that I can bring home to my family. I can even be hurt or killed by the people I am trying to help. And nobody cares; it's passed off as just being part of what I signed up to do. The really funny part is, I don't remember EVER signing up to be hurt or killed. I wanted to help people and make a difference in the world... stupid, huh? Now, I am just a name and credential on a line of the work schedule. Would I have become a nurse if I had known then what I know now? I'm really not sure."

The stark voice of the future came through loud and clear not so long ago. It is always enlightening to gain a bird's eye view of what is down the road from where we are currently standing. This panorama was painted for me when I spoke with a medical resident at the beginning of the COVID-19 pandemic. I asked if she found that there was much support for the frontline medical staff. She said, "Yes, people have been very grateful and generous. In the beginning, it was great, how much food was delivered for the hospital workers, and how people kept thanking us for being there. I question how things will change when the excitement of

COVID-19 wears thin. Before the pandemic hit, lots of days were real shit shows with waves of sick and hurt patients lined up for hours. Nobody seemed to care about us then. I just wonder if they will still remember us when the furor about the pandemic dies down."

I would be remiss to leave you on such a bleak note. We all understand that our healthcare workers are struggling right now. They are the foundation upon which our healthcare system is precariously balanced. My goal is not to disempower you by diminishing your strength and determination; but to help you, both consumers and healthcare workers, move forward to advocate for yourselves.

Throughout my nursing career, I have participated in multiple mandatory educational requirements. Annually, I have learned more than any nurse ever wanted to know about how to fight fires. You see, fires are deadly serious business when they occur in a healthcare setting. Of all of the overwhelming information that was taught on a yearly basis, there was one very key piece of wisdom that I have always kept close at hand in case of an emergency. When fighting a fire using a fire extinguisher, aim at the base of the blaze. Intuitively, people want to direct efforts to the flames on the top; they are, seemingly, the most dangerous and ought to be addressed first. I have learned that this is not necessarily the case and will not help to efficiently put out the fire; it may actually serve to spread the flames outward. It was drilled into the fledgling group of reluctant healthcare firefighters that we must always remember to focus our attention on the base of the conflagration and, with perseverance, the flames would be controlled, damage minimized, and injuries prevented.

How does this relate to the inferno happening currently in healthcare? I, like many of you, make my way through life as a visual learner. This image gives me perspective. Perspective allows the opportunity to gain a bit of traction in focusing on how to contain the flames that are raging out of control in the current healthcare culture.

For those who are consumers of healthcare, focus on the base of the fire where the frontline healthcare workers and patients are located. Ask questions. Read up on current issues in healthcare. Mindfully discard your assumptions and pay attention to facts. Use what you have learned in this book as a launching pad to assist you in constructing your action plan. Actively engage in building a healthcare culture that works to promote health and healing.

And, for those who work in healthcare, take a breath. Give yourself the space and grace to take inventory of your own physical, emotional, and spiritual health. Perhaps there are burdens and experiences that you continue to carry and ignore. Take time to acknowledge your discomfort. After taking the time to sit in the pain for a bit, move on working on healing.

What is your first step? I have worked hard to open the door for action; it's up to you to walk across the threshold. Take a look back at the suggestions I have written in the previous chapters. Find stillness, self-nourish, soothe your soul, connect with an old mentor, or find your voice about an issue that affects you and those you care for on a visceral level. These are just a few options to assist you in gaining momentum. Be kind to yourself and your colleagues. And, remember that it is okay to ask for a little help. I have faith in you. You can do this!

Acknowledgments

It is with a heart full of gratitude and wonder that I begin this "thank you note." Writing a book of any type is a challenging endeavor, and I have learned while writing this one that support blended with regular portions of constructive criticism were key and unmissable ingredients, aiding and encouraging me to finish this project.

Along the way, I have constantly felt humbled by the kindness of others, especially by those who have strategically provided those important elements.

I am grateful to those who, graciously, have taken much time from their lives to speak to me about their painful and personal workplace violence experiences. To these people, I say that your candor and authenticity in the face of retelling horrific episodes are inspiring, and I cannot tell you how much I appreciate you sharing stories that are both painful and traumatic. Thank you, too, for allowing me the honor of sharing these same stories with my readers; you are all so brave—my heroes.

My writing experience for the last several decades has primarily consisted of checklists and nursing progress notes, and so I found the challenges of crafting prose to flesh out the ideas in this book more than a little intimidating. Fortunately, however, I have found myself blessed with what amounts to a small village of people who have shared with me their gifts of technical know-how and skills.

Writing coaches, editors, proofreaders, and graphic design artists have all played an important role in getting this book into the readers' hands.

I am so grateful for the help, guidance, patience, and wisdom of all these professionals! You have not only demonstrated talent in your chosen fields, but also provided assistance with grace and empathy.

Finally, to my family, friends, and healers:

I also cannot thank you enough for your relentless love and support while I have been learning—and continuing to learn—to navigate this new version of life, the one born after being assaulted in the workplace.

Not surprisingly, it has proved to be excruciatingly hard work to write about the subject of healthcare workplace violence. Having the safety net securely held in place by those who love me has been integral to getting through all the tough spots. I could not have done it without you!

Photo by: Melissa LaRose Photography, LLC

A life-long Northern New Englander, June Zanes Garen has spent over three decades on the frontlines of nursing. After surviving a violent physical assault in her workplace, she has become an advocate for healthcare workplace safety.

For more information and resources,
please go to:
heyicouldusealittlehelphere.com

CPSIA information can be obtained
at www.ICGtesting.com
Printed in the USA
BVHW070753270521
608292BV00001B/146